W9-AXE-612

PLAN OR DIE!
10 KEYS TO ORGANIZATIONAL SUCCESS

Timothy M. Nolan, Ph.D.
Leonard D. Goodstein, Ph.D.
J. William Pfeiffer, Ph.D., J.D.

Jossey-Bass
Pfeiffer
San Francisco

Library of Congress Cataloging-in-Publication Data

Nolan, Timothy M.
  Plan or die: 10 keys to organizational success/Timothy M. Nolan, Leonard D. Goodstein, J. William Pfeiffer.
  p. cm.
  Previously published under title: Shaping your organization's future. (previous ISBN 0-888390-327-X)
  Includes index.
  ISBN 0-88390-377-6 (hc.)—ISBN 0-89384-207-9 (pbk.)
  1. Management. 2. Strategic planning. 3. Organizational change. 4. Organizational effectiveness. I. Goodstein, Leonard D. II. Pfeiffer, J. William. III. Nolan, Timothy M. Shaping your organization's future. IV. Title.
HD31.N565 1993
658.4'012—dc20   92-51082

Printed in the United States of America.
Printing   3 4 5 6 7 8 9 10

Published by

350 Sansome Street, 5th Floor
San Francisco, California 94104-1342
(415) 433-1740; Fax (415) 433-0499
(800) 274-4434; Fax (800) 569-0443

Visit our website at: http://www.pfeiffer.com

Outside of the United States, Pfeiffer products can be purchased from the following Simon & Schuster International Offices:

Prentice Hall Canada
PTR Division
1870 Birchmount Road
Scarborough, Ontario M1P 2J7
Canada
(800) 567-3800; Fax (800) 263-7733

Prentice Hall Professional
Locked Bag 531
Frenchs Forest PO NSW 2068
Australia
61 2 9907 5693; Fax 61 2 9905 7934

Prentice Hall/Pfeiffer
P.O. Box 1636
Randburg 2125
South Africa
27 11 781 0780; Fax 27 11 781 0781

Prentice Hall
Campus 400
Maylands Avenue
Hemel Hempstead
Hertfordshire HP2 7EZ
United Kingdom
44(0) 1442 881891; Fax 44(0) 1442 882288

Simon & Schuster (Asia) Pte Ltd
317 Alexandra Road
#04-01 IKEA Building
Singapore 159965
Asia
65 476 4688; Fax 65 378 0370

PLAN OR DIE!

Contents

PREFACE

We first began writing about the need for organizations to commit to shaping their future in 1985. At that time, we saw both a varying need and a varying awareness of the necessity for change from organization to organization. Some industries were more evidently in need than were others.

Today, however, few organizations do not feel an intensified need. Competition for customers and resources is increasing, while companies are feeling less sure of their future. Not-for-profit and governmental organizations are also feeling more stress; the need for their services is up—and continues to rise—while resources to meet these needs decline. For all types of organizations, international trade issues are becoming more important.

Chapter 1 outlines the challenges that confront most organizations. It is candid because we believe the time to be subtle is past.

Nine of the ten keys to successfully shaping your organization's future are discussed in Chapters 2, 3, and 4. These nine keys come from the authors' work in this arena over the past twenty years. Shaping an organization's future is both an art and a science. These nine keys help to simplify and provide structure to a process that can feel *most* complicated and amorphous.

Chapter 5 provides the tenth key—doing Applied Strategic Planning. This method of strategic planning organizes the previous nine keys and increases the likelihood that they will be successfully implemented. Applied Strategic Planning is a process that is being successfully employed, worldwide, in over a thousand organizations.

Chapter 6 asks readers to examine the barriers that are relevant to their particular organizations, and it provides direction on how to overcome these barriers. The final challenge of this book is to make a commitment to shape your organization's future.

We thank those who have contributed to this book. This includes the many leaders and members of the organizations we have served over the past two decades. They opened their organizations to us; and while we endeavored to make them better for this exchange, they contributed to our understanding of what makes organizations succeed— and what is needed to shape their future.

It is hard to express adequately the thanks due Mary Kitzmiller, the Managing Editor. Her unique blend of expertise in the content of this book, her talent as an editor, and her perpetually positive attitude contributed greatly to the quality of this book. Also, the wit and artistic skill that the illustrator, David Hills, brought to this book are most appreciated.

We are interested in your reactions to this book. If you have comments or suggestions, please contact us through the Applied Strategic Planning Institute, 808 North Grand Avenue, Waukesha, WI 53186; telephone (414) 786-4700.

Timothy M. Nolan
Milwaukee, Wisconsin

Leonard D. Goodstein
Washington, D.C.

J. William Pfeiffer
San Diego, California

1

SHAPING YOUR ORGANIZATION'S FUTURE: THE MANAGERIAL IMPERATIVE

Let's talk about frogs. Frogs are very adaptable creatures. They can live on land or in the water, and that's not all. Frogs can adapt to hot arid climates, cold arid climates, hot humid climates, and cold humid climates. From a biological perspective, the frog has survived the ages because of its remarkable adaptability to the environment. But before we say hooray for adaptability, let's take a look at an aspect that surfaced during some experiments with frogs.

In a laboratory, frogs were placed in shallow pans of room-temperature water. They were free to jump out of the pans at any time. Under each pan was a Bunsen burner, which heated the water very gradually. As the temperature rose, degree by degree, the frogs adapted to the new temperature. Unfortunately, regardless of how hot the water became, the frogs never became uncomfortable enough to jump out of the pan. In fact, they stayed right there until the heat was so intense that the frogs died. Now *that's* adaptability!

Some of us, also, are incredibly adaptable. In fact, a major reason for our success as human beings is our ability to adapt. When we find ourselves, as individuals, mildly dissatisfied with our jobs, with our significant other, or with almost any other circumstance in our lives, we proceed to adapt. For many of us, the more our environment challenges us, the harder we try to adapt to those changes.

Organizations also tend to replicate the frog's approach to life. The tendency in most organizations is to make lots of smaller, gradual, adaptive changes in response to the changing environment. The frog's survival requires the ability to realize at some point that it is getting into "hot water" and needs to stop adapting. The frog needs to jump out of the pan—into the unknown—and move into a new, safer environment. So, too, must individuals

A Very Adaptable Creature

and organizations determine in a timely fashion when to quit adapting and to proceed with changing directions and finding environments more supportive to them.

The Need for Change

The need for organizations to change has never been greater than we see today. The challenges most organizations are facing in the 1990s and beyond do not lend themselves to success through adaptation. That's because the very rules under which business is being done are shifting rapidly, markets are changing quickly, and customers are demanding more and more. We examine some of these changes here and show why adapting will not be a sufficient response to them.

Unwieldy Size

The long-held concept within Western organizations that "bigger is better" is now in question. Some of the largest corporations (General Motors and IBM among them) are experiencing deep trouble. Their largeness, which in the past gave them market dominance, efficiencies of scale, and the ability to compete almost unfairly with others in their marketplace, no longer works in their favor. In fact, their largeness makes them less able to respond to changes in the marketplace. As a result, the quality and competitiveness of their products lag behind those of others who are smaller and more flexible.

Post-Cold War Changes

The early 1990s have become a new post-war period. At the end of each of our previous major military engagements, the U.S. domestic economy was strongly affected by the reassignment of resources and national priorities. This is also the case as the Cold War comes to an end.

The significant decline in the threat from the former Soviet Union has resulted in a radical shift in the defense industry, which will have a pervasive impact on the economy over the next decade. While the United States looks forward to the potential savings in military expenditures that this involves, whole industries that had been put in place to create the necessary weaponry for the Cold War are much less necessary. This means a massive loss of high-paying jobs, now unneeded high-quality production capacity, and some significant short-term pain for those directly affected.

The military itself will need less personnel, which will result in reductions in both the civilian and military work forces in each branch of the military. These reductions will, in turn, create more unemployment while ultimately freeing up human resources for applications to nonmilitary needs. The role and design of the military itself must be reinvented.

Increasing Global Competitiveness

There are also numerous indirect effects of this somewhat more subtle "post-war" period. For example, U.S. allies during the Cold War have also been relieved of most of the threat they felt from the Soviet Union. During the period of threat, they needed the United States to contribute to their protection. With the Soviet Union no longer perceived as a threat, countries such as Japan and Germany, which have been strong but somewhat constrained economic competitors with the United States, are now less militarily dependent on the United States and, therefore, much more willing to be outspoken and direct in their economic competition with America. This has led to a more open disdain for the United States and its large businesses. It is quite likely that international economic competition will accelerate in both breadth and intensity as a result of this post-war freedom.

Outdated Organizational Structures

Organizations are finding that many internal structures currently in place do not work effectively. The hierarchical structures that have been used to organize large numbers of workers and managers tend to be outdated. These structures were originated to facilitate the gathering and upward flow of information within the organization. The widespread use of computers has made these ponderous information-gathering, collating, and recording mechanisms unnecessary.

Furthermore, the hierarchy was originally set up to enable top managers (whether generals, church leaders,

CEOs, or executive directors) to make decisions that could then be transmitted downward through the organization. In this era of rapidly shifting markets and the need for decentralized decision making, such a structure is much less effective.

For an organization to be responsive, more decisions must be made by those nearest to—and best informed about—the challenge at hand. Less decision making must come from the CEO. There is a significant need to develop new organizational structures that are more responsive to the challenges of the 1990s.

Faster Cycle Time

Time has become a new competitive domain. An organization that seeks to be responsive to customer needs must develop ways to create a product or service more quickly. The norm in automobile manufacturing used to be a seven-year period from conceiving a new vehicle to making it available in the showroom. To the truly customer-responsive organization, this delay is unacceptable, since the customers who were queried about their wants and needs are long gone by the time the product is delivered.

To increase customer responsiveness, production cycles have been shortened dramatically, resulting today in a span of approximately two years from concept to actual product. In fact, the norm in even heavy manufacturing has shifted toward one of constant improvement, which by definition means that every time an improvement is made, a new and better product is the result. Thus, the responsiveness of the producer has become much greater in most businesses and industries. Achieving faster production cycles requires radically rethinking the way in which work is done. Failure to do so means the organization will be left out of the competition and runs the risk of becoming a boiled frog.

Shifting Quality Expectations

In the past, only a limited percentage of customers for most products and services expected to receive top quality. This limited group of consumers also expected to pay a premium price for these top-quality products or services. The price expectations are less and less present in the 1990s. Now virtually everyone expects top quality, often at whatever price is paid! Organizations that hope to compete by providing a low-cost, lower-quality product or service are thus in great danger as customer expectations shift.

Virtually every organization must examine not only how to maintain current levels of quality but also how to establish mechanisms that will assure constant improvement of the quality of the products and services. This necessity has created great stress in organizations that have not had to deal significantly with this critical dimension in the past. Reducing this stress requires dramatic change, not mere adaptation.

Accelerated Changes

Change in our world is not only certain, it is occurring at an accelerating pace. In fact, more than 80 percent of our technological innovations have occurred since 1900. Furthermore, it is predicted that the last fifteen years of this century will see as much technological change as the first eighty-five years. Figure 1-1 lists many familiar items that have come on the scene during the twentieth century. Many people living today can remember when these things did not exist. Within the next decade another list of such "necessities" will emerge—a list so different from anything we have now that we cannot even predict it.

Air conditioners	Latex paint
Air travel	Magnetic tape
Antibiotics	Paperback books
Automatic transmissions	Personal computers
Automatic washers and dryers	Polio vaccine
Birth-control pills	Refrigerators/freezers
Compact discs	Running shoes
Credit cards	Smoke detectors
Detergents	Supermarkets
Disposable diapers	Synthetic fabrics
Fast foods	Television
Frozen foods	Transparent tape
Health insurance	VCRs

Figure 1-1. Some Items Not Generally Available a Few Decades Ago

During the nineteenth century, few people could even imagine life as we live it today. In 1899 Charles H. Duell, director of the U.S. Patent Office, thought the Patent Office had run its course and should be abolished. In his view, "Everything that can be invented has already been invented."

It sometimes is tempting to believe that we now live in a similar age and have reached the limits of technological change and that nothing more is possible. Yet those who study the clues to the future are convinced otherwise (Naisbitt and Aburdene, 1990; Cetron and Davies, 1991). They believe that what is past is prologue and that the task of choosing and managing the future is still with us. In fact, given the turbulence of our times, the task of shaping the future is *the* managerial imperative of the 1990s.

Competitive Environments in Flux

The way businesses are organized, governed, and affiliated is also in a constant state of flux. In the early 1990s, new business start-ups reached almost 750,000 annually in the United States. While many of these businesses will fail, many will "go public" and become the large corporations of the future. Additionally, mergers, acquisitions, and buy-outs have been and will continue to be a way of life. This means that competitors will constantly be reshuffling and reconstituting themselves. They will enter and leave markets based on a variety of agendas.

In the early 1990s, both IBM and GM announced their determination to invent new futures for themselves, landing each on the cover of *Business Week.* The business press is full of stories describing how much-smaller firms are shaping their futures—recreating a U.S. steel industry, creating new applications for technology, and shaping the service industries.

The organizations involved in mergers, acquisitions, and buyouts must compete while going through these significant changes, which can be a real challenge. Those with whom these organizations do business, or with whom they compete, must also quickly respond to these changes in the competitive environment. Any one of the situations we have described here would push the need for organizations of all sizes to shape their own future. When several of these change factors are working in concert, such an organizational effort is critical.

A Quick Look at Your Organization

Our discussion of change elements has probably been on target for your own organization on some dimensions and off target in other aspects. The questionnaire in Figure 1-2 (see page 11) is provided to give you an opportunity to do a quick review of your own business environment. Take a few minutes to answer the questions.

Every organization should be *proactively* shaping its own future—that is, actively shaping rather than attempting to adapt to identified future scenarios. Having responded to the questions in Figure 1-2, you should have a quick subjective picture of what your organization is facing as you commit to shaping its future.

If low numbers (reflecting low concern) are the correct answers for your organization in all four questions, then—in the frog analogy—your organization is in relatively cool water. This means that your efforts to shape your organization's ideal future can be more leisurely paced than they could if you were experiencing high levels of concern.

If, on the other hand, you circled high numbers (reflecting high concern), your organization may be in great danger; you—like the frog—may be experiencing an environment that has moved past cozy warm to dangerously hot. In that case, the process of shaping the future must be very intense and very focused if your organization is to survive.

If your answers are between the two extremes, then you are likely experiencing water that is becoming warmer, and—like the frog—you need to deliberately speed up the process of shaping your organization's future.

This quick analysis is subject to all of the blinders that occur when one is dealing with significant threat. In answering some of the questions, you might have understated your concern simply because doing otherwise would have been too frightening. Understatement also results if you have done insufficient analyses in key areas to be aware of the true level of threat. On the other hand, you might have overstated concern because of your approach to change. The main point to remember is that to be successful in the long term, you must make a commitment to shape your organization's future—starting now!

1. How well assured are our sources of income (revenues, grants, sales, etc.) for the next five years?

1	2	3	4	5
Not Concerned (Well Assured)				Highly Concerned (No Assurances)

2. What level of competition can we expect for our current customers and markets over the next five years?

1	2	3	4	5
Not Concerned (Expect Little Competition)				Highly Concerned (Expect Extreme Competition)

3. What level of change is taking place in our industry?

1	2	3	4	5
Not Concerned (Extreme Stability Assured)				Highly Concerned (Dramatic Change Likely)

4. Do we have the time, personnel, and financial resources to make required changes quickly and effectively enough to maintain or surpass our current levels of success?

1	2	3	4	5
Not Concerned (Have All Resources Required)				Highly Concerned (One or More Resources Very Limited)

Figure 1-2. How Hot Is the Water in Which Our Organization Operates?

Blocks to Shaping the Future

If the acknowledged need for organizations to shape their futures is so high—if the organizations' members are feeling the heat—why aren't more organizations successfully shaping their futures? The reasons lie both inside and outside the organization. Externally, the limits on successfully shaping the future are closely linked to (a) increasingly tough competitive environments that, in some cases, seem unforgiving of error and (b) a highly fickle stock market that tends to push management toward a short-term view.

Inside the organization are even more restrictions on shaping its future. These include the following:

1. Inertia caused by a history of success
2. A lack of conceptual skills
3. Outdated planning approaches
4. A lack of leadership
5. Avoiding risk-taking decisions
6. Declining resources
7. Limits on flexibility
8. Lack of empowerment

External Blocks

Tough Competitive Environments

In more and more industries, the competitive environment has heated up dramatically. The quality of competitors' products and the push toward constant improvement of goods and services have greatly increased the level of competition. As organizations examine their own place in a given market, they must acknowledge that the competition is not standing still but rather is seeking to take increasing portions of the market share. Additionally, more and more markets are becoming unforgiving of those who fall short of customer expectations. In this era, major airlines go out of business and major department stores declare bankruptcy. While new business start-ups are at all-time highs, so are business failures. This environment—while encouraging organizational leaders to search for a new and more viable future—does not allow much room for mistakes.

Fickle Stock Market

Another complicating factor for today's organizations is a stock market that places too much emphasis on short-term results and allows limited latitude for investing in the future. This situation has a negative impact on virtually all publicly traded corporations, as well as on those new businesses that aspire to do their own initial public offering.

The process of shaping an organization's future requires both investment and moving in new directions and, therefore, carries with it inherent risk. While the risk of not moving into new and potentially more productive directions is obvious, stock analysts tend to focus on the risks involved in creating the organization's ideal future. More important, however, most senior managers *believe* that these limits exist in the stock market. Given this perception, they tend to remain conservative, believing it safer not to acknowledge the need for change or to leave current, well-established markets for markets with a higher potential.

Internal Blocks

Inertia Caused by Success

One of the factors most likely to block an organization from effectively shaping its future is a history of success in achieving its current business goals. This history of success often creates an inertia that is difficult to break. Stakeholder resistance to changing what has been successful provides a "safe" reason not to proceed with shaping the future. However, this success might have occurred in an era when it was easier to achieve. The 1960s and 1970s continue to influence decisions in the 1990s, especially for not-for-profit or governmental organizations. During that long-gone era, resources were plentiful and most organizations could feel successful. Now—even though resources have declined and success is more difficult—the memories remain strong.

Success was also easier in the past for many for-profit organizations. At the close of World War II, 75 percent of all the world's production was concentrated in the United States. U.S. organizations, therefore, have a long history of dominance in manufacturing in the world market. Since then, the U.S. market share has steadily eroded; however, it was for many years offset somewhat by constant growth in domestic markets. Many organizations were able to increase market share easily or at least predictably.

Success was achieved despite relatively sloppy business approaches. For example, in the late 1980s and early 1990s, U.S. businesses were "discovering" quality as a new business issue and saw customer service as "breakthrough thinking." Candidly, to "discover" quality and customer service and report it in the business press is analogous to publishing an article in an educational journal "revealing" that reading would be a good skill for young children to learn!

Organizations that have had easy success find it difficult to take control, to make the hard decisions necessary for shaping their futures, and to manage their plans with sufficient rigor to change their visions into reality. Too much success in the past can blind you and your organization to the increasing temperature of the water and the risks of parboiling.

Lack of Skill in Conceptualizing

Many managers lack conceptual skills. Managers at any level need technical, human resource, and conceptual skills. These skills, however, need to be distributed in different patterns for various levels of management. First-line supervisors need considerable technical competence and human resource skills and just a bit of conceptual skills (see Figure 1-3).

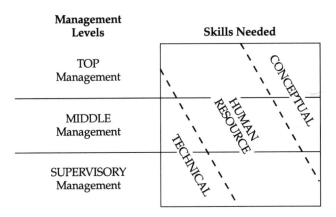

Figure 1-3. Management Skills

Middle managers need less technical knowledge, a bit more human resource skills, and a good deal more conceptual skills. Senior managers need few technical skills but a great amount of conceptual skills.

Management training has focused on increasing human resource skills, while the need for improving conceptual skills has been largely unmet. In fact, most managers are trained and educated for years in their technical skills (accounting, engineering, marketing, and so on), for hours in human skills (one-half day here and there in topics such as communications and conflict management), and almost not at all on how to think and manage conceptually. The result has been too many senior managers and other organizational members who are not skilled at thinking strategically. Although this skill is critical to shaping the organization's future, people tend not to do what they are not good at doing. Strategic conceptual thinking is a clear requirement to avoid joining the legion of boiled frogs.

Outdated Planning Approaches

Where markets are not rapidly changing, the future of an organization is often seen as a linear extension of the past. The planning approaches used in this situation project the future in a manner much like an electronic spreadsheet on a personal computer. Given this type of environment for many Western organizations—whether governmental, not-for-profit, or operating with a profit mission—the planning technologies that have emerged have been much more linear than those that could serve virtually any organization in today's rapidly shifting business environments.

A strong undercurrent in leadership circles is toward the idea that strategic planning does not work. To the degree that the approach to strategic planning is more like long-range planning—simply projecting the future—this claim is probably true. A major block to shaping the future is the need for a technology that enables the organization to create a vision of its ideal future and then to put into place those strategies and tactics necessary to fulfill that vision.

Lack of Leadership

Another block to shaping the future is lack of leadership in the organization. Instead of taking control, establishing a vision of the ideal future, and focusing the organization's resources on achieving that targeted vision, leaders often find themselves unsure of what to do. The result can be an embarrassingly naive approach that may even result in blaming others inappropriately for a problem. For example, when U.S. automotive executives traveled to Japan with President George Bush in 1992, Robert Stemple, CEO of General Motors, immediately upon his return was quoted as saying, "They're just not fair. Japan does not want to share. They want the whole market." To assume a willingness to share a market is naive; it reflects an inability to grab hold of the situation and move it in directions favorable to one's own organization. This attitude can block the successful shaping of an organization.

Risk Avoidance

Senior managers in organizations today tend to put almost inordinate energy into avoiding taking risks. A huge amount of organizational effort is put into checking and rechecking assumptions prior to making commitments. In a competitive environment that asks for timely, effective decisions, this is a major constraint on achieving success. As the water heats up around more and more organizations, the larger risk may be in *not* taking dynamic steps—in not effectively shaping the organization's future. The new question becomes "Are we *failing* enough?" This question reflects the need to learn by doing, which involves making mistakes. If the organization can create an expectation of trying new things and *learning* from its efforts, whether the effort succeeds or fails in the moment, it will enhance the likelihood of shaping a future that will ensure long-term success.

Declining Resources

More and more organizations are experiencing a significant decline in the availability of resources—financial, human, physical, and technical—with which to create the future they desire. This decline is often correlated with an increase in the temperature of the water surrounding the organization. In other words, as the organization experiences declining levels of success in doing business the same old way, its dollar reserves dwindle. For example, U.S. automobile manufacturers lost over $11 billion in 1991, thus reducing dollars available for shaping their futures. Critical human skills and talents decline, or people may depart the organization completely. Physical resources are not kept up to date through investment and are thus less able to support a dynamic movement toward the future. Finally, technological resources decline, since they, too, require constant nurturing and investment. The net result is that many organizations that want to shape their future are unable to turn the vision into reality because they lack the necessary resources.

Limits on Flexibility

In an environment where timely decisions are necessary and quick action is required, organizations must be flexible if they are to achieve their ideal futures. Unfortunately, many organizations of every size have become inflexible. Decision making requires moving the problem and solution through layers of managers. In the typical hierarchy, the manager at each level is empowered only to say "no" to a given proposition. Often the only affirmative action available to that manager is to move the decision on to another layer of the hierarchy.

This decision-making process is wholly inadequate for the realities of the 1990s. The largest organizations in the United States are dramatically affected by their lack of flexibility. Both IBM and General Motors (GM), in their efforts to create a future that is positive and desirable, have acknowledged that their structures lack flexibility.

Despite the fact that GM was losing over $1.5 million every day of 1991 (a total loss of $4.5 billion), top management took no decisive action until shortly before Christmas, when it announced a downsizing of 74,000 people. One index of the size of this loss is that GM would have lost approximately $10,000 in the time it took you to read that last sentence! Industry analysts and others agree that what GM must eventually do is dramatically restructure the entire company and completely change its marketing approach. Instead, what GM is doing by its downsizing is slowly adapting to the ever-increasing water temperature, surely running the risk of becoming a boiled frog.

It is not only large organizations that have determined that they have been too inflexible to serve their markets. Medium-sized and smaller organizations have also found it necessary to take dramatic steps to increase their ability to be responsive. For example, Norwest Banks, with a heavy midwest-U.S. presence, has made it possible for branch managers to make loan decisions independent of any loan-review committee for loans up to $10 million. Such flexibility in the normally conservative banking community is unusual and comes in response to the need to create a system that holds people accountable, gives them responsibility, and is predicated on a large degree of trust. This is simply the requirement if an organization is going to be truly customer responsive.

Lack of Empowerment

As organizations in the 1990s examine what it will take for them to have long-term success, it is clear that the only competitive advantage an organization carries toward the year 2000 is its people. Unfortunately, while an organization's human resources are a critical variable for success, these same resources constitute one of the major blocks to achieving the organization's ideal future.

While the business literature in the early 1990s carries a prevalent theme of the need for empowerment of workers within organizations, the lack of empowerment is an equal-opportunity affliction in too many organizations. Not only do lower-level workers not have a sense of empowerment, all too often it is also lacking in senior management. The managers' caretaking role, instead of a leadership role, may be the most devastating block to the organization's efforts to shape its ideal future.

If people believe that they cannot succeed, they are invariably correct. (Unfortunately, the inverse is not true; that is, self-confidence alone cannot ensure success.) An organization in which the "cannot" attitude prevails, especially among senior managers, will find itself unable to shape its ideal future.

What Is Needed to Shape an Organization's Future?

Discontinuous Futures

With rapid technological and social changes come discontinuous futures. Suppose, for example, that your company had been a producer of vacuum tubes for radios. Becoming a manufacturer of transistors would *not* have been a natural progression, because a vacuum-tube company could not readily adapt to manufacturing transistors. Nor could a transistor company adapt to producing silicon chips. Suppose, furthermore, that your company was the world's most efficient producer of vacuum tubes, with the highest-quality tubes, the lowest production costs, and the most humane working conditions. All of these things would make no difference, because—except for some rare uses—the vacuum tube would no longer be a needed product. And making the changes from vacuum tubes to transistors and from transistors to silicon chips involve such different technologies and different mind sets that each of these steps would constitute a discontinuous future, as did the shift from buggy whips to electromechanical starters. Figure 1-4 illustrates this concept of discontinuous futures.

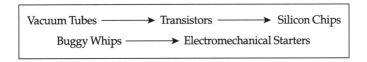

Figure 1-4. Examples of Products Involving Discontinuous Futures

Think of a public utility that controls thousands of miles of high-voltage transmission lines. In twenty to forty years, most experts agree, there will be no more high-voltage lines. Energy may be beamed from a mountain top or from outer space. Then the power company will be in the real-estate business, trying to dispose of thousands of miles of property that is only 300 yards wide. Furthermore, the glut of copper from the unused lines will reshape another industry or two!

A drastic change has also occurred in the healthcare market. The movement toward outpatient treatment and outpatient surgery is changing the whole industry. One hospital, unable to fill its rooms with patients, quit trying

Miles and Miles of 300-Yard Property

to adapt all its facilities to treating the sick and turned the top floor into a hotel for those visiting the patients in the hospital. Other hospitals have turned otherwise unused wards into substance-abuse and adolescent-treatment centers. Unlike the frog, these hospital managers jumped out of the pan and went in another direction—well *before* it was too late to act.

What we see in these examples are discontinuous futures in which changing technologies and changing human needs will require organizations to make quantum leaps to use those technologies and to meet those needs. Life in the future is going to be so different that we cannot even predict it, much less adapt to it. More and more, organizations will be faced with an end to the business they have thought themselves to be in and a need to chart a new and rather different future. When the County of Los Angeles Public Library embarked on strategic planning some years ago, it had to deal with questions such as "Will books exist in the year 2000?" and "Will the community library be a continuing viable public service?" These are the types of questions that we believe all organizations and their leaders should be asking.

It is necessary to ask these sometimes frightening questions in order not to be vulnerable to rapidly changing market conditions. These questions are also important in scanning for positive opportunities that otherwise might have been overlooked. The increased comfort that comes from dealing with discontinuous futures might result in a reconceptualization of the overall business, a timely phaseout of a declining line of business, or entry into new high-potential lines of business.

Skill to Achieve the Vision

If there ever was a time—and we doubt that there was—when we had a need for managers who were not leaders, and leaders who were not managers, that day is gone forever. We must have managers who also have a sense of vision, and we must have leaders who have a sense of management. Figure 1-5 illustrates the different mixtures of management and leadership. Someone who is high in leadership and low in management is merely a dreamer—someone with a great vision but without the planning and managing capacity to bring the dream into reality. A person high in management and low in leadership is just an administrator—someone who is great in executing a set plan in an orderly world. It takes someone who is high in both management and leadership to be a complete leader, and the future requires such a blending of both skills. To complete the quadrant, we can see that a person low in both skills would be an abdicator—someone who can neither dream nor manage.

Leadership

		Low	High
Management	High	Administrator	Complete Leader
	Low	Abdicator	Dreamer

Figure 1-5. The Management-Leadership Quadrant

Complete leaders need to constantly monitor their competitive environment and carefully position their organization to become a leader in a market. This sometimes requires entering the market through the back door or, as some have dubbed it, by offering a Trojan horse. For example, the Apple Computer people knew they had to reach beyond the desktop-publishing market to create a niche for their product (Sculley and Byrne, 1987). Their sales department went after the aerospace corporations and other industries that could buy the Macintosh for engineers and designers. Once the systems were in house, they began to be used for other computing purposes as well. Soon all the other employees wanted the user-friendly Mac for their own tasks.

Strategic and Tactical Decisions

The difference between strategic decisions and tactical decisions is the difference between "what" and "how." Strategic decisions determine *what* an organization will do— the leadership task—and tactical decisions determine *how* it will be done—the administrator's or manager's task. Most senior executives earned their positions by knowing the how, not the what—by being tacticians or managers,

The Important WHAT Question

rather than being strategists or leaders. However, good tactical solutions alone will *not* prevent you from joining the ranks of the boiled frogs.

Therefore, a real challenge in the strategic planning process lies in changing managers into leaders, so they can begin to think in terms of the what instead of the how, especially when the whats are new or perhaps not currently known. This is why conceptual skills (mentioned earlier) become so critical as one advances into more and more responsible positions in an organization.

If an organization makes the strategic decision that it is "going to Maine," numerous tactical questions must be answered: How are we going to get there? By plane, car, automobile, bicycle? By walking? What gear do we pack? Which route do we take? Where do we stop on the way?

Those tactical decisions, however, are much easier when we know the strategy—*that* we are going to Maine. If we did not know whether we were going to Maine or London or Mexico City, the tactical questions would be virtually impossible to answer. Perhaps we know we are going to Maine, but we do not know *when*. A trip to Maine in June will require answers quite different from those for a trip in December.

Although both strategic and tactical decisions are critical for success, we need to be clear on both *where* we are going and *how* we are going to get there. The Applied Strategic Planning process provides a practical approach for developing that clarity (Goodstein, Nolan, and Pfeiffer, 1992). We define Applied Strategic Planning as *the process by which the guiding members of an organization envision its future and develop the necessary procedures and operations to achieve that future.* The operative words in this definition are "guiding members," "envision," and "procedures . . . to achieve that future." In Chapter 5 we discuss this process and make these operative words real.

Ten Keys to Successfully Shaping Your Organization's Future

After extensively studying organizations that have been successful and after becoming virtual coroners of organizations—investigating what went wrong, what caused the fatal heart attack—we have come up with ten managerial imperatives (which we call "keys") to successfully shaping an organization's future. Opposite is a list of these keys; the next four chapters provide an in-depth analysis of them.

Key:		**See Chapter:**
0→ Key 1	Base decisions on values.	2
0→ Key 2	Have a mission based upon a shared vision.	2
0→ Key 3	Sound a rallying cry and persevere.	2
0→ Key 4	Promote and reward risk taking.	3
0→ Key 5	Empower people — all of the people.	3
0→ Key 6	Create and nurture a learning organization.	3
0→ Key 7	Encourage innovation and flexibility.	4
0→ Key 8	Monitor and manage "down board."	4
0→ Key 9	Maintain a market focus.	4
0→ Key 10	Conduct Applied Strategic Planning.	5

In Conclusion

The need for organizations to take control and to shape their own future is significant. For more and more organizations, the water surrounding them is heating up dramatically. The rules are changing almost faster than they can be understood. As you examine your own organization and your desire to shape its ideal future, you may identify a variety of challenges facing you over the next decade. Although the logic of an organization committing itself to shaping its own future is solid, unfortunately the number of organizations who are successfully doing so is still far too small. This is due to a wide range of both internal and external blocks to shaping the organization's future.

This book will help you examine what it takes to shape your organization's future. It presents you with concepts and processes that will guide you toward shaping your ideal future. It will, if necessary, help you chart a new course so that your organization will see the need to jump out of stagnant or threatening situations and into ventures more compatible with the rapidly changing environment. It will help you to avoid becoming a boiled frog.

2

CULTURE, VALUES, AND IMPLEMENTING VISIONS

In a small village in ancient China an old, old man had a magnificent vision. His great vision was for the village to have its own real, live, honest-to-goodness, fire-breathing dragon. The old man said over and over, "If we had a dragon in our town, our children would behave. If we had a dragon in our town, the feudal government would give us more benefits. If we had a dragon in our town, people would come from many miles away to see the dragon, and our economy would soar." And on and on and on. He described his vision to everyone he saw, and he talked about it so frequently that eventually it became the vision of everyone in the village. In fact, everyone was saying, "If we only had a dragon, all our problems would be solved."

Upon hearing all this, the gods of the dragons said, "Hey, these people really want a dragon. And if any group of people in the whole history of mankind ever deserved a dragon, these people deserve one!" So, lo and behold, one morning the old man walked out of his house, and there—standing right in front of him—was a real, full-sized, honest-to-goodness, fire-breathing dragon.

The old man took one look at the dragon and was so stunned that he fell over with a heart attack and died. This, in turn, startled the dragon so much that he roared and spewed flames all over the village, which proceeded to burn to the ground.

The moral of the story is: There is a helluva big difference between a vision and its implementation.

Organizational Visions

Many contemporary organizations have similar dragons. "If only we had an infusion of cash!" "If only we could get rid of Joe (or Mary)!" "If only we could get this product

The Helluva Big Difference

into production!" "If only we had this!" "If only we had that!" While having a vision is important in guiding an organization, it is imperative to differentiate between dreams of magical solutions and a vision of what the organization could be. For us, a vision is not an idle dream of magical solutions to today's organizational problems. Rather, it is a clear image of what an organization could and should become if it is to realize its full potential. Such a vision provides an organization and its members with a picture of how things could be—what the Promised Land looks like—and a sense that it is possible to arrive there safely.

The vision is the foundation upon which the organization's mission is built. It serves as an energy source for all the organization's stakeholders. The vision should provide a template by which the organization can analyze external threats and opportunities. Furthermore, the vision should help the organization to organize and focus internal resources to bring the vision into reality.

From where do such visions come? Typically, they come from the organization's leadership, most often from the CEO. If the CEO will not or cannot articulate such a vision, it is that person's responsibility to find it in the organization or help develop it. It can come from the executive group as a team, from the organization's board of directors, or from any top executive who has been able to infect others with his or her enthusiasm and ideas. But, whether or not the organization's leader is the one principally responsible for the creation of the vision, that leader has the responsibility to package and sell that vision, so that all members of the organization can understand it and commit themselves to bringing that vision into reality. The leader must make certain that the vision has visibility and that it is kept alive and vibrant in order to maintain its energizing properties. Kouzes and Posner (1987) have strongly argued that managing the visioning process and its implementation is *the* central task of leadership.

Even if a person agrees that a vision has this potential for organizational impact, he or she may not understand where it belongs in the day-to-day operations of the organization. Thus, the vision must be clearly articulated in the organization's mission statement, a topic to which we will return later in this chapter. The vision must also be present in the minds of all the organization's significant stakeholders. It should serve, at least in part, as the basis for every important decision made by the organization; that is, each important decision should be prefaced by "Does this advance our vision?" The answer should explicitly and implicitly shape the day-to-day activities—and thus the future—of the organization.

Steve Jobs, founder of Apple Computer, provides a clear example of a how a vision helped shape the development of an organization when he describes the early days of Apple: "There's something going on here . . . something that is changing the world, and this is the epicenter." Who would not be excited by such a vision and who would not want to be part of the epicenter of world change? Such visions, which contain both directing and energizing aspects, are unlike the fantasies of magical solutions raised in the dragon parable at the beginning of this chapter. What is needed is not an idle fantasy, but a clear, powerful vision that arouses and sustains the actions necessary for that vision to become a reality.

Such visions are not confined, however, to high-tech organizations. Richard E. Snyder, president and CEO of Simon & Schuster, a well-established New York-based publisher, has a vision of changing his traditional company from a publisher of general-interest books (sold in bookstores and other retail outlets) into America's largest educational publisher. He manages by setting long-range strategies and setting bold objectives—objectives that initially seem impossible to achieve; but he provides both the energy and the resources that enable others to achieve those goals.

For example, his vision entailed investing over $60 million in becoming the first truly modern large publisher in an industry where the use of typewriters was common and computerization of the office was slow. Under his leadership, Simon & Schuster has used computers and specially designed software that allows writers, editors, marketers, financial analysts, attorneys, and book designers to simultaneously work on a project, enormously shortening the total cycle time needed to produce a book. The better production scheduling, lower composition and revision costs, and capability to quickly develop customized textbooks have allowed Snyder to raise his company's expected profit margin from 10.9 percent in 1990 to 15 percent by 1994—all in an industry where single-digit margins are typical.

But visions are not enough. A tremendous gap often exists between an organizational vision and its current reality. A central problem thus arises: How can the organization successfully bridge this gap? Specific plans need to be developed and successfully implemented before the vision can become a reality. Those plans, however, can be developed and executed only within the cultural context of the organization. Without understanding organizational culture in general and the culture of one's own organization in particular, converting the vision into reality becomes virtually impossible. Thus, understanding organizational culture has become part of the first managerial imperative.

Organizational Culture

An organization's culture provides the social context in and through which the organization performs its work. A *culture* is a pattern of assumptions and beliefs deeply held in common by members of an organization (Schein, 1985). One important assumption is how the organization relates to its environment: submitting, dominating, harmonizing, or finding a safe niche. Another is how the organization handles facts and discovers truth: through revelation from the top of the organization, through management consensus, or through broad participation. Still another is how it views human nature: Are humans seen as naturally good, bad, or neutral? How should they be treated? What is the "right" way to treat people? While we could go on in this vein, these examples should help you understand the nature of basic assumptions and how they provide the foundation for an organization's activity.

These assumptions or beliefs in turn give rise to *values*—end states of being—that are cherished by the members of the organization. Many people are aware of such company values as "honesty" or "loyalty," but they might never have realized that these values stem, for example, from assumptions about the usefulness of debate or about management of the natural environment. Values in turn give rise to *behavioral norms* ("the way we do things around here") that are evidenced in overt behavior and artifacts.

We can see the behavioral norms, with an occasional glimpse of the values, but we can only infer the assumptions and beliefs, which is one reason that it is frequently difficult to understand the culture of an organization. Figure 2-1 provides a graphic representation of this approach to understanding organizational culture.

It should be clear from Figure 2-1 that each of the three major elements—basic assumptions, values, and behavioral norms—affects the others. For example, basic assumptions shape values, but values over time can modify the basic assumptions. Similarly, values shape norms, but changing norms can affect values, and so on. None of these elements are static; they change slowly over time as the organizational culture deals with the ever-changing environment.

As an example of the importance of understanding and managing organizational culture, consider the case of British Airways (BA). In 1983 BA had lost $900 million (in U.S. dollars), was losing market share, and was generally noted for unreliable and generally poor service. BA's new CEO, Colin Marshall (now Sir Colin), was determined to turn the company around and make BA "the

---

BASIC ASSUMPTIONS (Taken for granted; invisible; difficult to decode)

    Relationships to the environment
        The physical environment
        The social environment, including the government
    Conception of human nature
    Relations among human beings

    ↓ ↑

VALUES (Indirectly measurable; held at a higher level of awareness)

    Measurable by social consensus
    Inferable from overt behavior

    ↓ ↑

BEHAVIORAL NORMS AND ARTIFACTS (Visible but require decoding)

    Overt behavior
    Stories, philosophies of operations, codes of conduct
    Documents, technology, physical structures

Adapted from *Organizational Culture and Leadership* by Edgar H. Schein, 1985. San Francisco: Jossey-Bass.

Figure 2-1. A Graphic Representation of Organizational Culture

World's Favourite Airline," his unlikely vision for BA. He quickly determined that the culture he had inherited was bureaucratic, authoritarian, and unresponsive—a product of its years of being owned by the government, managed by ex-military officers, and structured like a bureaucracy. The behavioral norms of managers were to avoid taking action, create a paper trail to cover themselves, and then wait till the crisis blew over. Only by facing the problems caused by this culture and taking on the responsibility of changing it was Marshall able to make BA a successful company (Goodstein and Burke, 1991).

Types of Cultures

Harrison and Stokes (1992) suggest that organizations can be regarded as having one of the four following orientations: (a) power, (b) role, (c) achievement, and (d) support.

The *power* orientation places most of the decision-making responsibilities at the top of the organization. Employees are expected to yield to leadership, to be loyal followers, and to understand that their leaders will be protective, generous, and indulgent in response to employee obedience. The *role* orientation is impersonal and requires employees to do what is required by the formal system. Emphasis is placed on rules and regulations and making certain that things are done "right." The *achievement* orientation is egalitarian, and all employees are seen as being able to influence those decisions that concern getting the job done. Individuals are able to use their authority to obtain the resources needed to complete the task. Organizations with a *support* orientation have as their goal the development of individuals. As such, the focus of the

The Paper Trail That Covers

organization is to help employees reach their own potential and to maximize their own learning.

This brings us to the first of our ten keys for successfully shaping your organization's future, as listed in Chapter 1:

Key 1
Base Decisions on Values

Rather than hoping for the arrival of its own dragon, an organization would be better served by conducting a self-examination directed toward better understanding what makes it really tick, the cultural base of its work. The primary focus should be on understanding the values driving the organization. Its members constantly make decisions while going about their work, and virtually all of these decisions are rooted in the organization's values and in the shared basic assumptions about how things work.

The notion that all organizational decisions are values-based is a difficult concept for many managers to accept; instead, they often insist that the value of the so-called "bottom line" drives all decisions. However, if we examine most organizational decisions, we will see that several different values underlie the creation of profits that can virtually always be decoded with careful study.

Consider, for example, the simple question of whether a company ought to be focused solely on making a profit or solely on growth. Most managers would quickly insist that neither of these two choices is a reasonable one and that some balance needs to be struck between them. Precisely! But what is the proper balance between profits and reinvestment in growth? Once we can agree that there really are other considerations besides profit (or growth), we are into recognizing the critical importance of values in decision making. Regardless of what balance is selected, the choice will be rooted in the values of the organization, not in a simplistic pursuit of profit.

As another example, consider the dilemma that many large service organizations have to face during a short-term economic recession. Something has to be done to reduce the number of employees on the payroll. Although that decision is based on bottom-line considerations, how it is to be implemented is clearly a values consideration. Will employees be laid off? If so, on what basis? Last hired, first out? Or will older employees be encouraged to retire early? Another alternative would be to reduce everyone's hours or to ask employees to volunteer for furloughs.

When faced with a potential loss of jobs, the New York State Division of Equalization and Assessment was able to involve its employees in developing a set of "win-win" solutions to offset these potential losses. For instance, several employees volunteered for unpaid furloughs, thus saving several jobs. This gesture not only demonstrated the employees' commitment to one another, but it also heightened their commitment to the organization and its future. Each such overt expression of the organization's culture heightens the members' awareness of the culture—and further "fixes" that culture.

The underlying value on which such decisions are based is the fundamental view taken of employees—of such human factors as loyalty, seniority, potential, and so on. In an organization that sees employees as disposable commodities, the decision could be quite different from that in an organization that views employees as invaluable human resources. The value generally placed on employees will determine how they are treated in the organization and how human resource policies are formulated.

Another value that is important in many— or most— business decisions is *risk taking*. Organizations range from being risk aversive, on one extreme, to risk seeking on the other, depending primarily on the value that senior managers place on risk. Risk-aversive organizations grow relatively slowly. They generally have personnel policies that protect them from litigation and employee complaints and are relatively low in innovation in both products and marketing. On the other hand, risk-seeking organizations frequently play "bet your company." For risk-seeking managers, much of the thrill of the game is in walking the tightrope between reasonable and excessive risks. Risk-aversive managers recognize that their strategy is unlikely to produce rapid change or rapid growth, but neither does it put the entire organization at risk.

Values as Organizational Anchors

An organization's values provide a useful anchor in an environment that is constantly in flux. As Chapter 1 pointed out, the rapidity of change in contemporary society provides a sense of uncertainty of direction and lack of clarity about the future. Organizations that have clearly articulated values and that behave congruently with those values will avoid the fate of the Chinese village whose dream of the dragon came true—much to the villagers' horror.

Some organizations work hard to articulate their values, typically in some kind of written statement that is ordinarily widely circulated in the organization. Examples are the Five Principles of Mars (see Figure 2-2), the Johnson & Johnson Credo (see Figure 2-3), and the Hoechst Celanese Statement of Values (see Figure 2-4). These statements, which have evolved over the years, represent the explicit values by which their managers and employees attempt to run these businesses.

---

1. **Quality**
The consumer is our boss, quality is our work, and value for money is our goal.

2. **Responsibility**
As individuals, we demand total responsibility from ourselves; as associates, we support the responsibilities of others.

3. **Mutuality**
A mutual benefit is a shared benefit; a shared benefit will endure.

4. **Efficiency**
We use resources to the fullest, waste nothing, and do only what we can do best.

5. **Freedom**
We need freedom to shape our future; we need profit to remain free.

Figure 2-2. The Five Principles of Mars

Developing this sort of explicit statement of values often proves to be a useful activity for a management team. It forces the team members to confront their own personal values and to determine the degree to which they are shared by others. These individual values then are blended into a credo or statement of operational values about how the organization should go about doing its work. It should be clear from what we have already said that these values have always implicitly driven the decisions of the organization. Making them explicit provides for a more conscious choice and allows managers to be directly guided by these values as well as to question them.

When nonproductive values overlap, collusion occurs. That is, the dominant values are widespread and do not lead to a functioning organization. Managers, for example, may agree that risk taking is to be avoided at all

Our Credo

We believe our first responsibility is to the doctors, nurses and patients,
to mothers and fathers and all others who use our products and services.
In meeting their needs everything we do must be of high quality.
We must constantly strive to reduce our costs
in order to maintain reasonable prices.
Customers' orders must be serviced promptly and accurately.
Our suppliers and distributors must have an opportunity
to make a fair profit.

We are responsible to our employees,
the men and women who work with us throughout the world.
Everyone must be considered as an individual.
We must respect their dignity and recognize their merit.
They must have a sense of security in their jobs.
Compensation must be fair and adequate,
and working conditions clean, orderly and safe.
We must be mindful of ways to help our employees fulfill
their family responsibilities.
Employees must feel free to make suggestions and complaints.
There must be equal opportunity for employment, development
and advancement for those qualified.
We must provide competent management,
and their actions must be just and ethical.

We are responsible to the communities in which we live and work
and to the world community as well.
We must be good citizens — support good works and charities
and bear our fair share of taxes.
We must encourage civic improvements and better health and education.
We must maintain in good order
the property we are privileged to use,
protecting the environment and natural resources.

Our final responsibility is to our stockholders.
Business must make a sound profit.
We must experiment with new ideas.
Research must be carried on, innovative programs developed
and mistakes paid for.
New equipment must be purchased, new facilities provided
and new products launched.
Reserves must be created to provide for adverse times.
When we operate according to these principles,
the stockholders should realize a fair return.

Johnson & Johnson

Figure 2-3. The Johnson & Johnson Credo

VALUES

Performance

- Preferred supplier, dedicated to understanding and meeting customer expectations
- Commitment to safety, employee health and protection of the environment
- Responsible corporate citizen
- Earnings to support long-term growth
- Consistently superior to competition
- Commitment to continual improvement

People

- Respect for individuals and appreciation for contributions each can make
- Diversity accepted and valued
- Concern and fair treatment for individuals in managing business change
- Equal opportunity for each employee to achieve his or her potential
- Employee pride and enthusiasm
- Informed employees through open communication

Process

- Openness and trust in all relations
- Innovation, creativity and risk taking encouraged
- Teamwork throughout the organization
- Participative goal setting, measurement and feedback
- Decision making at the lowest practical level
- Actions consistent with clearly understood mission and long-term goals
- Recognition for quality achievements
- Resources committed to ongoing training and development

Figure 2-4. Hoechst Celanese Statement of Values

costs, not recognizing that risk avoidance may be the most risky strategy of all, given the nature of our current "hot water" environment.

When productive values do not overlap, individuals with different values can constantly push to have their positions heard and worked out in the equation of decision making. For example, one of our clients, a computer peripheral factory, never has enough completed units ready for shipment to meet its production quotas. It regularly faces the choice of not meeting its schedule or sending out equipment that has not been completely tested. The plant's quality-control staff argues vehemently that the plant should not ship any equipment that has not been properly "burned in," while the manufacturing group—eager to meet its production schedule—argues that it knows that the equipment has been satisfactorily manufactured. Such nonoverlapping differences exemplify a situation in which an organization makes the difficult decision not to openly clarify values.

A simple technique for further understanding the organizational consequences of value differences is presented in Figure 2-5. In Quadrant 1, a shared, productive value might be "We will build this organization for the long run." A commitment to such a value can become the basis for the thoughtful investment of resources. In Quadrant 2, two seemingly opposed values, such as "We should maximize profits" and "We should grow into new markets," can and should become productive if these differences are successfully managed though open, balanced discussions that serve as the basis for developing a consistent, clear direction for the organization. A Quadrant-3 value that could become nonproductive is "We must grow!" Such an imperative can blind an organization to other values-based options that should be considered. In Quadrant 4, if one senior manager believes in valuing employees while another values high productivity, this *can* lead to a disagreement between them on virtually every business decision. Such disagreements are nonproductive if each manager seeks to maximize his or her own position,

		VALUES	
		Similar	Different
ORGANIZATIONAL CONSEQUENCES	Productive	Quadrant 1	Quadrant 2
	Unproductive	Quadrant 3	Quadrant 4

Figure 2-5. Organizational Consequences of Similar and Different Values

further polarizing the situation with no compromise or understanding possible. Each encounter becomes a costly one for the organization.

These nonproductive, nonoverlapping values simply produce chaos and conflict. Members of the organization fight, even though winning the fight would have little or no consequence. Furthermore, such conflict dissipates much of the creative energy of the organization and leaves little for constructive work.

Making Values and Behavior Congruent

The fact that an organization's behaviors need to be congruent with its values unfortunately presents a problem for many organizations. For example, a company that prides itself on customer service received a telephone call from a customer complaining that a driver had accidentally run over and ruined a toy as he backed out of the customer's driveway ("Managers' Manager," 1987). The manager went out of his way to buy a duplicate toy—for $2.67—and delivered it in person. But when he turned in the bill for reimbursement, the company refused to pay. Clearly, the values articulated by the company simply were not reflected in the procedures that should have enabled employees to carry out behaviors congruent with the stated beliefs. Employees quickly recognize such inconsistencies and adjust their behavior accordingly—often at a long-term cost to the organization. It is unlikely, for instance, that the manager in this company will again display as much creativity in responding to other customer complaints.

Successfully shaping an organization's future requires its leaders to recognize and articulate those values that drive its decisions and to disseminate them throughout the organization—the first of our keys to successful strategic management. Not only do these values have to be disseminated, but individual members of the organization need to feel empowered to make decisions that make those values real. Without this congruity, members of the organization feel that the articulated values are fraudulent, and they become alienated.

As an example of congruence between behavior and espoused values, look again at the list in Figure 2-2. M&M Mars is one of the largest privately held companies in the world. Throughout the company—whether in Singapore, in Waco, Texas, or at the head office in the U.K.—these five principles are prominently displayed. A story is told about a buyer employed by Mars who was able to secure cacao beans from a distressed grower at a figure well below the market price. He returned to the company expecting to be lauded for the money he had saved Mars. Much to his surprise, he was disciplined, and the contract was rewritten at a higher price. He was told that Mars valued its suppliers too much to take advantage of them during a depressed period and, furthermore, that Mars could someday be the distressed party and would want reciprocal treatment. This action was congruent with the company's value of mutuality (Principle #3).

Another example of congruence came to our attention when one of the authors of this book noticed a hole in a two-year old suit, purchased at Nordstrom—a department store legendary for its commitment to customer service. He took the suit back to Nordstrom to ask if it could be rewoven. To his amazement, the sales clerk located a suit exactly like it, altered it, and presented it in exchange for the old suit without additional cost! While Nordstrom might have lost some money on that particular transaction, we told and retold this story countless times before publishing it here—providing Nordstrom with the kind of favorable publicity that no money can buy. And Nordstrom made at least one of us a lifelong customer as well.

Key 2
Have a Mission Based Upon a Shared Vision

The second key to successfully shaping an organization's future is having a mission that is based on a shared, clearcut vision of the organization's future. Earlier in this chapter we pointed out the importance of having a vision—how it can provide direction, drive, and determination to organizational members. But too often visions are fuzzy or poorly articulated and lack action plans. A well-articulated mission statement can remedy this lack of clarity and specificity. A well-crafted, readily understood mission statement can serve as a template to guide the organization to its desired future. Mission statements are actionable visions!

Individuals throughout the organization need to understand what business the company is in and how its values drive that business. Without such widespread understanding, employees will not develop much commitment or loyalty to the organization and its success. A well-thought-out mission statement can create this understanding. The dominant thrust of the organization needs to be stated simply enough for every employee to understand it and to behave accordingly. One example is the clearly stated mission of Domino's Pizza: "Pizza in thirty minutes." This statement does not suggest that Domino's aspires to make the best pizza in the world or that it makes gourmet pizza. It simply says, "If you want a pizza in a hurry, call us." This mission statement also encourages Domino's employees to meet that challenge. There is high clarity in the goal of delivering a pizza in thirty minutes, a clarity that every person who works in the organization—from the order taker to the pizza maker to the delivery person, as well as supervisors and managers—can understand.

An American hotel chain provides a similar lesson in clarity of mission: "Hospitality that brings guests back." The company recognizes in this mission statement that the way the guest is treated is the key ingredient in gaining repeat business, which is vital in the highly competitive hotel business. This mission statement provides a template for the behavior of the entire staff. Each time an employee of this chain has an encounter with a customer, he or she can ask, "Did I treat this customer in a way that will increase the probability that he or she will use our hotels again?"

Ambiguous Missions

In contrast to these clear mission statements, many organizations apparently prefer ambiguous missions—either because the ambiguity does not require individuals to be accountable or because it frees them from having to make the decisions necessary in creating a clear direction. Whether or not a pizza has been delivered in thirty minutes is easy to determine, and employees can be held accountable; but statements such as "providing quality" or becoming "world class" are vague enough to protect employees and their managers from accountability. Ambiguous mission statements put the organization at grave risk.

It is often asserted that an organization's mission is too nebulous to define neatly in a few words. However, if the mission cannot be clearly stated, the organization will have no way to determine when and if it is accomplished.

The Value of Ambiguity

Although not all missions can be as sharply defined as "pizza in thirty minutes," organizations must be able to articulate their goals in a straightforward fashion—one that all employees can understand and to which they can all relate. When managers argue that doing so is not possible or even attemptable, we must ask if this is really the case or if perhaps they prefer the ambiguity—and lack of accountability—that results from failure to address the issue of mission clarity.

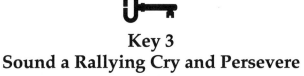

Key 3
Sound a Rallying Cry and Persevere

A third key to successfully shaping an organization's future is to sound a clear rallying cry—that is, to make a statement that directly involves and energizes people throughout the organization to achieve the corporate mission. An old apocryphal story illustrates the usefulness of a rallying cry. Three bricklayers were working side by side. When asked, "What are you doing?" the first bricklayer said, "I'm laying bricks." The second one answered, "I'm working to feed my family." The third worker, who obviously had a higher degree of commitment, responded, "I'm building a cathedral."

The early work of the National Aeronautics and Space Administration (NASA) provides another illustration. In an interview, a janitor at one of the major NASA installations portrayed his job as "helping to put a man on the moon." Like the cathedral-building bricklayer, he was involved in and energized by a task that transformed the actual work being done into an achievement that was greater than what the individual alone could produce.

Rallying cries are ways to bring people to a commitment to the vision that they share. The loss of this kind of captivating vision is undoubtedly one factor involved in the more recent decline of NASA as an organization. The envisioning process, coupled with strong management that provides constant rallying on the work-unit level, produces the kind of commitment that makes for strategic success and obviates the need for close supervision.

In another recent example, a U.S. computer manufacturer used breaking the barrier of a billion dollars in sales as the rallying cry for the year. "Break the billion-dollar barrier" was seen on corporate banners, on corporate shirts, on lapel pins, and in other conspicuous places, and it involved every part of the organization. Employees clearly understood that breaking this barrier would put them in the major leagues of computer manufacturers. Productivity and sales increased until the billion-dollar mark that the company targeted was substantially exceeded in the year of the rallying cry.

Commitment

Organizations are often ineffective in producing a mission statement specific enough to energize employees toward successful change. There is no real rallying cry.

Before reading further, look at the mission statement in Figure 2-6. This statement is so vague and so general that you wonder what the product is and, indeed, what the industry is. As you read it, ask yourself if it might not be equally appropriate for your own organization. It may come as a surprise to you to learn that it is General Motors' corporate mission statement, developed by senior executive staff over a period of many months and at a cost of many thousands of dollars in staff time and facilities. While there is nothing "wrong" with this mission statement, there is little right about it. That is, it is so general that it has neither the clarity to hold people accountable nor the rallying cry to produce the commitment so vital to the success of an organization. While we would certainly not suggest that drafting a more dynamic mission statement would resolve the organization's current problems, its bland, unfocused quality does suggest that GM's top mangers apparently do not appreciate the need for a strong, shared vision of a desired future state—the need for a rallying cry.

The fundamental purpose of [this Corporation] is to provide products and services of such quality that our customers will receive superior value, our employees and business partners will share in our success, and our stockholders will receive a sustained, superior return on their investment.

Figure 2-6. Sample Mission Statement
of a Real Organization

Clarity is a necessary but insufficient precursor to commitment. Managers, both by what they say and—even more important—by what they do, must demonstrate the importance of the mission statement to shaping the organization's future. Managers must articulate the mission on a regular basis, indicate how their day-to-day decision making reflects the importance of the mission statement, use mission-related criteria in the performance appraisals of employees, and do whatever else they can to clearly communicate their commitment to the mission. Only by such exemplary behavior can the necessary rank-and-file commitment to the mission be achieved. Once it is obtained, however, it has the capacity to energize the entire organization in a new and profoundly different fashion.

Perseverance

As already noted, change does not occur easily. Even with the best conceptualized and planned change effort, even with the clearest rallying cry, perseverance is still necessary. A further analysis of the change process will help explain this need for perseverance.

Change can be made at four different levels:

1. The knowledge level
2. The attitude level
3. The individual-behavior level
4. The group-behavior level

The important variables at each level are (a) the difficulty in making the change and (b) the time it takes to make the change (see Figure 2-7).

It can be quick and easy to make changes at the knowledge level. To change attitudes takes longer and is more difficult. Changing individual behavior takes even longer

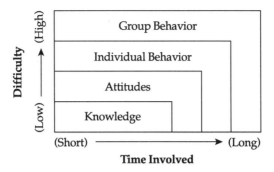

Figure 2-7. Change in an Organization

and is increasingly more difficult. Finally, it is extremely difficult and may take a very long time to change group behavior. Therefore, for change at the group and organizational level, perseverance is necessary.

In many organizations we hear the expression, "We've tried that twice (or three times) and it doesn't work here," which brings to mind the 147/805 Rule.

This rule is based on two facts: (1) The Wright brothers failed 147 times before they built an airplane that would fly, and (2) Thomas Edison failed 805 times before he found a workable filament for the electric light bulb. The learning to be internalized from this rule is that to achieve success, one must persevere. Where would Edison and the Wright brothers have been had they stopped after their first 10 or 20 attempts? This is an easy rule to forget in today's "hurry-up" marketplaces.

An organization's most dynamic change strategy lies in its methods of rewards and sanctions. If you are going to change an organization in a lasting way, you must change rewards and sanctions. You must reward people when they do it right. Remembering the 147/805 Rule will take you far. In Pogo's language, "Life is full of unsurmountable opportunities."

3

CHANGING ORGANIZATIONS AND PEOPLE

This is the way a beehive operates: A worker bee finds a major source of pollen, flies back to the hive, and performs a dance that shows the other bees the direction of the pollen source. The speed of the dance indicates the distance of the find from the hive.

Then the queen bee gives the word, and out of the hive fly the workers directly to the newly found pollen. At least, 85 percent of them do. The other 15 percent don't follow the swarm. They appear not to have comprehended the message and go wandering off in other directions. And what happens to this 15 percent? They look for other sources of pollen, and when they find it the story starts all over again.

The Other 15 Percent

One time after relating this parable we were asked, "Did you know that the mortality rate is higher for the 15 percent than it is for the rest of the hive?" Our answer was yes, but the survival of the hive as a whole requires that level of sacrifice and commitment. Being part of that 15 percent in human organizations typically means that the majority 85 percent try to hammer you into shape—to entice you to join them in their everyday routine and to stop taking risks, wasting time searching for new products or markets, or scouting out new opportunities.

However, for any organization—human or otherwise—to be effective and survive, it must recognize the value of the behavior of this courageous 15 percent and, in fact, reward that type of behavior. A strong common denominator in successful organizations is that they all find a way to get some of their members to take a risk—to try something new and different, to scout out the trends of the future. If an organization is too tightly structured to allow this kind of deviant behavior, if every bee is required to go to a previously identified source of pollen, there will be no research and development, no attention paid to the long-term future, and—all too often in this era of rapid change—no future at all.

Resistance to Change

One of the morals of our bee parable is that avoiding the adaptation trap always requires some effort in scouting out new directions, new alternatives, new sources of pollen before it is too late. Taking off in these new directions to find new sources, however, often requires both organizational and personal changes—and there generally is a strong resistance to change, both on the individual and organizational level.

Change is in the eye of the beholder. If the beholders have initiated the change, then it is "logical," "rational," and "well thought out." If the beholders perceive the change as being done *to* them or if they disagree with the change, it is illogical, irrational, and improperly conceived. How many people do you know who were delighted at a change that put their jobs at risk? And how many do you know who refused an organizational restructuring that increased their scope of responsibilities, and, not incidentally, their remuneration?

The Need for Homeostasis

We can see resistance to change as an effort to maintain *homeostasis,* or the status quo, which is almost always seen as more comfortable than an unknown future brought about by some unasked-for change process. One of the strongest human motives is the drive toward homeostasis. To accommodate this drive, organizational change needs to be carefully planned and managed.

Individuals vary in their appreciation of the need for change and in their tolerance for accepting change, and these differences are important to consider in planning any organizational change effort. It appears that each person has an optimal need for change or variety. If the amount of change in a person's life is less than optimal, the person will intentionally seek a change or some variety. If, on the other hand, there is too much change in a person's life, he or she will strenuously resist any additional change.

Organizational change efforts that follow long periods of stability are less likely to be resisted than those that follow periods of turbulence. And even after periods of stability, there will be some individuals who are low in their appreciation of the need for change who will resist that change and be rather intolerant of efforts to advance that change.

Reasons for Resistance

We may wonder why—if some change is necessary and desirable to human existence—organizations encounter so much resistance to change as they seek to shape their future. The reasons are many; among them are the following:

1. The reasons for the change have not been clearly communicated.
2. The new goals or objectives have not been accepted.
3. People fear the unknown.
4. People fear failure in a new situation.
5. People prefer the present situation.
6. People have no confidence in the person proclaiming the change.
7. People support an alternative change goal.
8. People support an alternative method of implementing the change.
9. People were not involved in planning the change.
10. The proposed change will interfere with already existing plans for change.
11. The new goals are irrelevant to many people.
12. There are many different perspectives on the problem—people see the problem differently.
13. The announcement of the proposed change provides an opportunity to oppose management or whoever is proposing the change.
14. Accidental misstatements during the planning process set off resistance. Humor is especially dangerous in this connection.
15. People see the proposed change as an attack on their performance and react defensively.

16. People resist leaving friends and familiar surroundings.

17. Timing of the announcement is wrong—or perceived to be wrong.

18. People see the change as positively affecting others, but see nothing for *themselves* in the change.

19. People resist this change even though it benefits them because they fear that the next change may have adverse consequences for them.

20. People fear having to learn a new job or having to work harder.

21. People perceive loss of status, rights, or privileges because of the change.

22. People resist change simply because it is *change*.

Managing Resistance

Understanding these—and the many other reasons for resistance to change—will help you anticipate resistance, attempt to identify its sources and reasons, and modify your efforts to manage that resistance to ensure the success of your change efforts. Specifically, we suggest that you consider the following tactics for managing resistance:

1. Involve all interested parties in contributing to planning the change.

2. Clearly articulate the need for change and the goals and objectives of the change process.

3. Prepare a written document setting forth these goals and objectives to reduce misunderstandings.

4. Address the individual needs of those who will be affected by the change; help people retain what they treasure wherever possible.

The Danger of Humor in Announcing Change

5. Have the people involved in planning the change announce the change.

6. Design flexibility into the change; include enough "wiggle room" to accommodate exceptions.

7. Allow for the completion of the current change before beginning the next change effort.

8. Design communication sessions in which those affected by the change can air their feelings about it early enough to positively contribute to the change process.

9. Be open and honest with people; accept the reality that there will be some negative consequences from the change, at least for some people. Be concerned with maintaining the trust of all.

10. Do not leave an opening to return to the status quo; do not announce decisions unless you are ready to move ahead with the changes.

11. Continually focus on the positive aspects of the change.

12. Do not attack those who resist the change. Be reasonable and accepting but resolute in your decision.

13. Continually look for areas of agreement between yourself and those who oppose the change and emphasize the agreement, not the differences that you have with them.

14. Be attentive to your calendar in planning the change. Avoid holidays and other sensitive times in announcing changes.

15. Clearly set out the boundaries of the change and attempt to avoid unrealistic fears about future, unplanned changes.

16. In planning the change, make changes that negatively affect rights, benefits, and privileges only as absolutely necessary.

17. Include adequate retraining and readjustment processes into the plans for change.

In planning and making significant changes in organizations, we need to strike a balance. We cannot afford to criticize those who are against change. In fact, resistance to change is an important part of maintaining stable organizations.

If things change too fast, disastrous things can happen in an organization. For example, Boise Cascade was initially focused on wood products production. It decided to vertically integrate, and the company went all the way from designing seeds to growing trees to building and selling houses. That is about as vertically integrated as an organization can get, but the plan did not work.

There was nothing intrinsically wrong with the idea, but its execution left a lot to be desired. Too much, too fast! Little or no attention was given to laying a proper ground-work, involving those who would be most affected by this massive change, getting adequate commitment from all the relevant stakeholders, and developing a comprehensive implementation plan. This story can be repeated again and again with different organizational examples.

The failure of this and other poorly thought-through change efforts is hardly surprising. We strongly believe that any change effort has to be *applied,* that the plan has to be implemented in order for the planning effort to be worthwhile. You must lay a proper groundwork, involving those who will be affected by the change, obtaining commitment from the relevant stakeholders—especially the organization's employees—and developing a comprehensive implementation plan—the steps typically neglected in most change efforts.

One of the well-documented psychological laws of organizational behavior is that involvement leads to commitment. Use a high-involvement approach to achieve a high commitment, a commitment that is essential for the success of the change effort.

Changing Goals

The process of comprehensive, planned change requires that organization members ask themselves some funda-mental questions, such as, "What business are we really in?" and "What business should we be in?" Effective or-ganizations have a high degree of goal clarity. In these organizations, the answers to these two questions are congruent, regardless of which employees are asked.

Major change efforts often require an organization to modify its goals and significantly change its mission in order to set off in a new direction to find a new source of pollen. Such changes in goals are usually the most difficult to accomplish as they usually create the maximum amount of resistance in the organization.

This resistance is not surprising if you think about it for even a minute or two. Changing an organization's mission or goals leaves virtually everything open to change, and everybody and everything is at risk. Small change efforts affect only a selected few, but modifying an organization's mission can affect everybody and thus must be especially carefully managed since the resistance can be expected to be widespread.

Changes in an organization's direction cannot be made if they violate members' values or the beliefs and assumptions that underlie the core culture. Those in favor of change can push, but the organization will not budge. Even when a lot of effort is put into the change, if it is contrary to the organization's value system, the organization springs right back, resuming its previous patterns.

The simplest and most useful approach to successfully implementing such directional changes is found in the work of Kurt Lewin (1975). His approach to organizational change involves a three-step sequence of unfreezing-movement-refreezing; that is, the organization must first unfreeze or break the patterns of the past, then move or try out new patterns, then refreeze or institutionalize those movements that have produced the desired results. Each of these steps must be carefully planned and managed.

According to Lewin, there are three different levels—individual, structures and systems, and climate/interpersonal style—at which this sequence *must* occur for success. Intervention techniques are necessary at each level if the planned change effort is to succeed.

At the unfreezing level, it is important to bring home the need for change. Public pronouncements by top management to share data about the precariousness of the present situation, obvious cost-cutting measures, downsizing, and the like serve to help unfreeze the organization.

Movement occurs through such processes as training, changes in organizational structures and systems, and team building. Refreezing occurs through the institutionalization of the changes and clear signals that a new level of organizational performance has been achieved.

The successful change efforts at British Airways illustrate Lewin's model. In 1982 BA lost US$900 million and was losing market share. Its management structure was hierarchical and nonresponsive. The British government decided to divest itself of BA and sell its shares to the public. A new CEO, Colin Marshall, was brought in with the goal of making BA "The World's Favourite Airline," a feat that required a substantial change of direction. But, using Lewin's model, the change was executed, and by 1987 BA's profit was US$435 million; today it is generally seen as a service-oriented and market-driven business. The resistance to change needed to be managed, and it was. Figure 3-1 illustrates how Lewin's model was used to explain the success of this change effort at BA.

Key 4
Promote and Reward Risk Taking

All organizational change involves risk taking. Yet such risk taking is rare in organizations. To get people to take

Levels	Unfreezing	Movement	Refreezing
Individual	Downsizing of workforce (59,000 to 37,000); middle management especially hard-hit. New top management team. "Putting People First."	Acceptance of concept of "emotional labor." Personnel staff as internal consultants. "Managing People First." Peer support groups.	Continued commitment of top management. Promotion of staff with new BA values. "Top Flight Academies." "Open Learning" programs.
Structures and systems	Use of diagonal task forces to plan change. Reduction in levels of hierarchy. Modification of budgeting process.	Profit sharing (3 weeks' pay in 1987). Opening of Terminal 4. Purchase of Chartridge as training center. New "user friendly" management information system.	New performance appraisal system based on both behavior and performance. Performance-based compensation system. Continued use of task forces.
Climate/inter-personal style	Redefinition of the business: *service*, not *transportation*. Top management commitment and involvement.	Greater emphasis on open communications. Data feedback on work-unit climate. Off-site, team-building meetings.	New uniforms. New coat of arms. Development and use of cabin-crew teams. Continued use of data-based feedback on climate and management practices.

Reprinted from "Creating Successful Organizational Change" by Leonard D. Goodstein and W. Warner Burke (1991), in *Organization Dynamics*, 19(4), 5–17.

*Figure 3-1. Applying Lewin's Model to the
British Airways Change Effort*

more risks, such behavior must be promoted and re-warded. Employees often have a formula in mind about risk taking: "When there's enough trust in the system, I'm going to take some risks." The trouble is that the formula is backward. The truth is that successful, productive risk taking results in trust. If people sit around waiting for trust to result in risk taking, they will be waiting a long, long time. Risk taking, when done and responded to properly, will create trust.

A story is told about an IBM employee who took a risk that cost IBM over $500,000. When he was called into the CEO's office, he assumed he would be fired. Instead, he was given a coveted assignment. He replied, "Naturally I'm very pleased but I'm also very confused. I cost this company more than $500,000, and you're giving me one of the real plum jobs in the organization. Why?" The CEO retorted, "We have just sunk a half-million dollars into your education, and we sure as hell are not going to pour it down the drain!"

Most companies, however, do not have that attitude toward risk. Indeed, it may have been too rare at IBM! Organizations do not typically say, "What's the positive side? What can we learn from what we've done wrong?"

Jerry Harvey (1988) tells a story of a Captain Asoh—a pilot of a Japanese commercial airliner—who depended on the power of forgiveness rather than the power of excuses or blame to clear himself of a major miscalculation. When Asoh descended too soon and landed in San Francisco Bay instead of on the runway, he set the plane down so gently that many of the ninety-six passengers were not aware of the mistake. At the National Transportation Safety Board's preliminary hearing about the incident, the press appeared en masse to witness the fiery testimonies and record the

The Learning Organization

numerous accusations. Attorneys for both sides in the case had leased hotel suites, expecting this to be a lengthy trial.

Captain Asoh was the first witness. According to Harvey, the first question was, "Captain Asoh, in your own words, can you tell us how you managed to land that DC-8 Stretch Jet 2½ miles out in San Francisco Bay in perfect compass line with the runway?" Although Harvey was never able to obtain an actual transcript of Captain Asoh's response, rumors say that he merely responded, "As you Americans say, Asoh f—d up!" With those words the hearing was quickly concluded.

Taking Risks

Not every system fosters a culture that allows employees to be completely frank and truthful. In most organizations mistakes are not tolerated, and the guilty are rewarded for hiding the truth. As Harvey reminds us, the person who has not made a mistake in the last year is also the person who has been afraid to try anything of significance. In these turbulent times, organizations cannot afford managers and executives who are afraid to try. If that is the case, they have to change their attitudes toward risk taking—or be replaced.

David Viscott (1977) identified six critical sources of risk. While his original work was focused on individual risk taking, these sources of risk have clear implications for organizational risk taking as well. The six sources are:

1. **Risks of growth**. Growth—both individual and organizational—entails risk, because it means that people will have to let go of current ways of doing things, possibly leading to failure.

2. **Risks of autonomy**. Autonomy involves the risk of having to accept responsibility for outcomes— for the future. Thus, autonomy can be fear arousing, especially if one has up until now been able to blame others or circumstances and thus avoid feeling responsible. A related risk comes from trying to be at one's best. Really trying can lead to a fear of success as well as a fear of failure. The latter is far more readily understood than the former. Success, however, is feared because it can raise the stakes and lead to future increased expectations, alienate one from friends, and otherwise disturb the smooth pattern of one's life.

3. **Risks of change**. As outlined earlier, the perceived risks involved in change arouse a number of both logical and illogical fears and a naturally following resistance.

4. **Risks of sharing and closeness**. While most of Viscott's observations in this area focus on risks in one's personal life, there are some organizational issues involved as well. For example, the current emphasis on autonomous and semiautonomous work teams requires a high level of trust and communication between and among team members. This situation can involve more openness and honesty than is comfortable for some members of the work team.

5. **Risks of control**. From our extensive consulting experience, both in organizations and in personal-growth groups, we know that most individuals continue to have unresolved feelings regarding control. This unfinished business may be left over from early relationships with parental figures—those who wished to control them—or from more recent experiences either in being controlled or in attempting to control others. These leftovers can lead to unexpected emotional reactions and thus need to be carefully managed when they appear.

6. **Risks of esteem**. Taking a risk can put the individual's self-esteem or an organization's reputation on the line. Only the most secure find this an easy risk to accept.

As indicated from this discussion, only a small portion of the reluctance to take risks in an organization comes from the obvious risk of losing money or being fired. If the organization is to achieve a culture that fosters risk taking, it must address the above issues. People must be made to feel secure in order to take risks. Insecurity leads to a fear of risk taking that stultifies organizations and prevents growth. The lack of success while taking a risk must not be labeled as a "failure," but rather must be seen as an investment in learning how to succeed.

Risk Management

Learning how to manage risks is an important part of creating an organizational culture that supports the shaping of the organization's future. Such learning must not be identified as too soft to be useful, but rather as strengthening the organization's resolve for creativity and innovation. Teams and individuals who are being asked to grow in their risk taking will need support, coaching, mentoring, and group skills.

A beehive that does not allow any of its members to search for new sources of pollen will not survive the year. Somehow the organizational culture has to grow to support greater risk if new sources of pollen are to be found and new lessons are to be learned.

Risk taking can be encouraged by modeling, but rewarding can promote it even more. Blanchard (1982) states it in one short phrase: "Catch people doing something right." There are few organizational behaviors more worthy of being "caught" than risk taking—for the good of the organization!

One side benefit of encouraging risk taking is a general improvement in the sense of empowerment throughout the organization. As people feel that they can take risks to move the organization forward—to find new sources of pollen—their ownership of the decision-making processes increases, as does their pride in the organization. Empowerment means that members feel that they are making a significant contribution to the development of the organization.

Key 5
Empower People—All of the People

Peter Block (1987) defines politics as the exchange of power, and empowerment is the positive way to be political. This means that empowerment is getting people to believe they are in charge of their own destiny, that what they do is going to influence the system; in other words, getting them to take a risk.

When people feel disempowered, their organization will start on a downward spiral that is difficult to stop. Employees begin to say, "What difference does it make what I do? I don't matter." This feeling can become epidemic in the system. Things that empower people in organizations become key elements in making a vital organization that can respond to change.

Stewart J. Leonard, CEO of Stew Leonard's—the Connecticut food store known for its commitment to customer service—loves to tell his tuna-sandwich story, which nicely illustrates the process of empowerment. It goes something like this:

> Every time I open my tuna-fish sandwich, one of these tubes of Hellman's mayonnaise falls out. My sandwich already has enough mayo and I never use the extra mayo, and it's real expensive. So I tell my deli manager to tell his people to stop with the extra mayo; it's unnecessary.
>
> Next week, I get my tuna sandwich and the damn mayo is still there. I call the deli manager to complain and he tells me that I've got to talk to Mary Eckstrand, who actually makes the sandwiches. When I call Mary, she tells me in no uncertain terms, "Sorry, Stew, but *my* customers want the extra mayo, so I'm going to continue to pack the extra mayo." And, you know my

reaction to Mary. Right on!! That's what I want Stew Leonard's to stand for.

We devoutly wish for more Stew Leonards and more Mary Eckstrands in organizational life.

In addition to the kind of power sharing exemplified by the Stew Leonard story, another thing that can be done to empower people is to acknowledge meaningful accomplishments. "Meaningful" is an important part of this, because if an employee is praised for something he or she knows is not significant, the praise seems like hogwash.

It is also helpful to ask for opinions and then really consider them. Some supervisors become trapped into thinking they are practicing participatory management just because they ask for opinions, even though they go ahead and do whatever they wanted to do in the first place. Managers need to listen to opinions, consider them carefully, and then make the best decision. Furthermore, those who offered suggestions need to be told how their input was used in the process, even if their recommendation was not followed. The employees need to know that they are helping to guide destiny, even when other courses of action are taken.

Elegant Currency

What is "elegant currency" with regard to empowerment? Elegant currency is a term applied to any act or object that one individual can easily spend that is highly regarded by the receiver. To one person, "Let's go have a beer after work" is elegant currency; to a person who wants to rush home, it can be a pain in the posterior. So the notion of "elegant currency" is not what is elegant to the person who is trying to empower but rather to the person who is to be empowered.

For some people, a letter of recognition is important and is framed and hung. For another, the letter is dropped into a drawer and forgotten. Competent supervisors know their employees well enough to determine the "elegant currency" for each of them.

Disempowerment

There are also ways people can disempower themselves. Block (1987) mentions five of them (see Figure 3-2). The first is by telling oneself stories about needing advancement before becoming empowered. For example, a person can say, "I'm going to start taking risks as soon as I get tenure," or "If I do that, it will get in the way of my advancement."

Deception about Advancement	Obsession with Approval	Selling Out for Cash
	Imagined Danger	Control at all Costs

Figure 3-2. Five Ways to Disempower Ourselves

Second, everyone needs approval—whether from one's supervisor, colleagues, or significant other. People need to seek approval. However, when they overdo this quest for approval, they disempower themselves.

Third, most people are driven by tangible rewards, especially money; but if they translate compliant behavior into ways to get paid, it disempowers them.

Fourth, people are motivated by a human wish to remain safe, but this also can be carried too far. Some people imagine that they are standing on the brink of the Grand Canyon, when in reality they are standing on a three-inch curb. They dare not step off the curb for fear of falling into the Grand Canyon. This perception of tremendous risk disempowers them.

The fifth way people can disempower themselves is by insisting on keeping control of the situation at all costs. Many senior managers cannot bring themselves to tell their employees, "I don't know," which they believe would be seen as losing control. Empowered managers, however, are willing to admit their lack of knowledge and say, "I don't know; we need to figure this out together." Without this kind of empowering, the willingness of the bees to seek out the new sources of pollen is significantly reduced.

Proactive Futuring

There are many ways of thinking about and planning for the future. Russ Ackoff (1981), one of America's premier strategic thinkers, has identified four such approaches.

1. Reactive, or planning through the rear-view mirror.
2. Inactive, or going with the flow.
3. Preactive, or preparing for the future.
4. Proactive, or designing the future and making it happen.

Reactive planning occurs in static organizations that dread the future because it means change. They await the return of their "golden yesterdays" and look to the future with nostalgia. Their strategic plans focus on how to pin down the pages on the calendar and hold off the sands of time. For many years, American railroads exemplified this approach with their policies of opposing change, especially the development of other modes of transportation.

Inactive planning simply means ignoring the need for planning and counting on muddling through. This high-risk, bet-your-company approach to preparing for the future is much more prevalent—and much more dangerous—than one might suspect.

Most organizations use some form of *preactive planning*. That is, they try to figure out what the future holds in store for them and then get ready. While this is an understandable approach, it is entirely too passive for our tastes.

Proactive futuring is the act of deciding what you want to happen and then setting out to make it happen. It is empowerment at the broadest level. John Sculley, Apple's CEO, says, "The best way to predict the future is to invent it." You have to imagine what you want and then take charge and make it come true. Proactive futuring enables the organization to have a future that would not otherwise have existed.

One of the best-known examples of this kind of proactive futuring is found in Procter & Gamble's development of Pampers. Their market research (that's what business organizations call their "scout bees") revealed that a major discontent of mothers was soiled diapers. Procter & Gamble saw that reducing this discontent would provide a new source of pollen and charged its product development staff with creating such a product. After considerable experimentation, Procter & Gamble was able to market Pampers, the first disposable diapers, a business now annually producing over $3 billion in revenues worldwide.

This kind of proactive planning—creating a new future for your organization, rather than waiting for the future to find you—is rare. However, in a rapidly changing environment, it is the best option offered for avoiding the Society of Boiled Frogs.

Key 6
Create and Nurture a Learning Organization

To succeed in shaping your organization's future, you must develop an organization that learns well, efficiently, and constantly. Such learning is critical, because competing in rapidly changing environments means your organization must be able to track your environments, identify changes, and adjust to these changes. You must try new things and determine what works and what does not work—increasing what does and swiftly abandoning that which does not. Then you must build a new cycle of learning upon this learning in a never-ending fashion. In the words of John Naisbitt (1990):

> In a world that is constantly changing, there is no one subject or set of subjects that will serve you well for the foreseeable future, let alone for the rest of your life. The most important skill to acquire now is learning how to learn.

This is as true of organizations as it is of individuals. Life cycles of products are shortening dramatically, sometimes ending prematurely and permanently as new products replace them. Organizations may also die, or at least decline severely, if they have not paid attention to the rapidly shifting demands being placed on them. The continued decline of General Motors over the past two decades in market share, revenues, and profits is but one case in point.

Many organizations are not doing well today because they simply do not change quickly enough to respond to their rapidly changing markets. They seem to have an "organizational learning disability" (Senge, 1990) stemming from fundamental flaws in organization design and management, poor job design, and deficiencies in the ways people in those organizations—especially managers—think and interact.

Negative Synergy

We have long observed in our consulting work that far fewer organizations achieve synergy than aspire to do so. The goal of synergy—in which the results of a group's efforts surpass those of its members individually—is one of the reasons underlying most mergers, acquisitions, and cross-departmental projects. The expectation is that two plus two will equal more than four. The reality is, all too often, that two plus two equals three or less! We call that negative synergy.

Why is this the case? On an organization-wide basis, negative synergy results from culture clashes between various units, lack of a shared vision, unclear missions, internal competition, poor communication, and inadequate leadership.

At the team level, similar negative factors are evident, although on a smaller scale. Value clashes replace cultural ones. Lack of clarity about the team's charter replaces lack of an organizational mission or an overarching organizational vision. In both situations, however, negative synergy is the direct result of being unable to learn and to improve performance efficiency as a result of this learning.

Developing Learning Organizations

Developing a learning organization requires a major commitment of time, energy, and resources. Within the organization, this commitment may mean examining and possibly changing social, financial, decision-making, and political structures. Risk taking will need to be encouraged. Communications throughout the organization will need to be improved, increased, and refocused. Resources will need to be invested in the development of a learning organization. A culture that nurtures a learning community will need to be developed and leadership will need to redefine itself.

Our experience indicates that most organizations do not take the necessary time out after having an experience to determine what they *can* learn from that experience, regardless of whether the experience is positive or negative in outcome.

How often does your organization take the necessary time after a new ad campaign, a new product launch, a failed hire, or whatever to really understand the factors that led to either success or failure and to discuss how performance in the future can be improved? Even when this evaluation is attempted, the focus all too often is on whom to blame or reward rather than on what everyone can learn from what has happened.

Structures currently in place in many organizations tend to inhibit such learning; hierarchical structures stifle the flow of information. These structures limit who can make what decisions. They are based on the premise that the whole organization is built to support the learning and the decision-making skills of those few at the top, not the entire organization. A learning organization must support learning among all of its members, and they must all be encouraged to take risks.

Learning and risk taking are two of the most important components of creating an organization that can successfully shape its own future. Such risk taking and learning mean that decision making must be more broadly distributed—empowerment. People at all levels of the organization must be expected to make decisions (including decisions that involve risks), observe the results, and learn from these efforts. Structures need to be developed to organize these innumerable learning opportunities while not stifling them.

To capitalize on this learning, communications must be dramatically increased. Communication patterns must be expanded beyond the bottom-up and top-down patterns typical in formal communication in hierarchical structures. To become a learning organization, employees must communicate in every direction, and everyone must be interested in what they are learning. It is necessary but not sufficient for individuals to greatly enhance their own levels of learning. The individual insights must also be readily available to all who might use them in improving their own work.

Improved, Increased, and Refocused Communications

Enthusiasm About Learning

A learning organization will emerge when the members become genuinely excited about the *process* of learning, because learning begets learning. A healthy curiosity will cause people to want to explore ways to do their work more effectively and efficiently.

Sometimes it is possible to build this interest in learning indirectly. For example, Johnsonville Sausage in Sheboygan Falls, Wisconsin, now funds *any* learning opportunity its workers find interesting—e.g., formal university or extension courses, archery lessons, photography, and so on. Enlightened leadership believes that if people get excited about learning topics of seeming irrelevance to their job responsibilities, this enthusiasm will increase their interest in learning on the job.

This plan has paid off dramatically for Johnsonville. It has grown to become the most profitable company in its competitive industry. This growth and sustained profitability come from workers who have become active learners, constantly seeking to improve both themselves and their company. These workers have created whole new businesses—for example, becoming subcontractors to larger companies—due to their industry-leading efficiency and constantly improving internal operations.

The Johnsonville Sausage example illustrates the power of a learning organization—one where everyone, not just those at the top of the organizational hierarchy, can learn to develop decision-making skills and have the opportunity to apply these skills. Bill O'Brien, CEO of the Hanover Insurance Company, has advised managers to redefine their jobs, "give up the old dogma of planning, organizing, and controlling," and "provide the enabling conditions for people to lead the most enriching lives they can" (Senge, 1990).

Creating and nurturing a learning environment requires a dramatic shift in the organization's pattern of decision making. It stresses the need to reorient the way people approach work. It requires investment; significant resources need to be allocated to this effort. The obvious forms of investment include course fees, travel, and other direct expenses of training and development. In a world where the half-life of a new engineer's knowledge is considerably less than six years and the half-life of the knowledge of a recent graduate in marketing is even less, there is a major need to replenish these declining resources.

Beyond the direct cost of education and training, however, there are even more critical investments to be made. People must be given time to explore new possibilities—to learn from their exploration. Managers must commit increasingly large portions of their time to nurturing the learning environment—listening, encouraging, coaching, and gathering and distributing new knowledge. They must also commit their most valuable asset—time—to learning and applying this learning themselves.

In the 1980s, Tom Peters made managers more aware of the importance of "Managing by Walking Around," of getting out of the office and interacting, observing, questioning, and listening. While Managing by Walking Around was not initially seen as a learning strategy, we believe that it clearly is.

Peter Drucker (1992) has pushed this notion one step farther in his encouragement of Managing by Walking Around—Outside. He advocates that mangers not limit their learning to internal issues, but that they wander around outside their own organization to learn what is happening in their environments, especially in their marketplace and with their customers. This is the ultimate goal of the learning organization.

The reason for creating and nurturing a learning organization is not to create an inner-focused university of people who enjoy learning with each other, but rather to keep the organization vital by having it learn how to better serve its markets and the customers that constitute those markets.

4

FROM VISION TO REALITY

Ayoung man watched his bride carefully prepare a turkey for their first Thanksgiving dinner. With great precision she snipped off the tail of the turkey just before placing the bird in the roasting pan. "Why did you cut off the turkey's tail?" he asked. "Oh," she shrugged, "you always cut off the tail before you cook the turkey." "But why?" he again asked. "Well, uh," she stammered, "my mother taught me to cut it off. I'll ask her when she comes."

With an innocent voice, the bride later asked her mother, "Why do we cut off the turkey's tail?" The mother exclaimed, "Oh, you should always cut off the turkey's tail!" "But why?" persisted the daughter. The mother then replied, "I learned it from your grandmother, and she was the best cook in the neighborhood. Many a time I watched her as she was preparing the turkey, so I would know exactly how to do it. Just before cooking it, she always cut off the tail. If you really want to know why, call her and ask her."

The bride made a long-distance phone call to wish her grandmother a happy Thanksgiving Day. Then she asked, "Grandmother, why do we cut off the tail of the turkey before cooking it?" The grandmother replied, "I have no idea why *you* cut it off, but *I* used to cut it off because my roasting pan was so small that a big turkey wouldn't fit unless I cut off the tail."

Our final parable addresses the issues of tradition and change. It illustrates how traditions can get established and how they persist—long after the needs they were developed to resolve have faded away. All organizations, including families, need to regularly reconsider their traditions, their well-established ways of doing business, to determine if they are cutting off turkey tails and what the costs and benefits of such actions might be. Without

The Chopped-Off Turkey Tail

such an intentional analysis and decision-making process, all of us can too easily continue to do what our grandparents or others started without understanding why or the costs involved. And the process of change requires innovation and flexibility.

Key 7
Encourage Innovation and Flexibility

Successfully shaping an organization's future, for the majority of organizations today, depends on the ability to be innovative. There is an important difference between creativity and innovation. Creativity involves generating ideas—creating options and identifying possibilities. Innovation, on the other hand, refers to applying those ideas, bringing them into reality. Unfortunately, many people, including many who should know better, have treated these two concepts as if they were equivalent. The terms have been used interchangeably and they should not be.

Creativity

Creativity, the ability to generate ideas that may be answers to a given challenge, is an important component of success in any organization. It is this flow of ideas that leads to the possibilities and opportunities for success. If you seek to develop a high level of creativity in your organization, you face a major challenge, because most people are far less creative than they could be. The formal educational system in the United States, for example, tends to suppress creativity. In an effort to organize the curriculum and the children, the system has evolved until orderliness is prized over creativity, and finding the single correct answer is the goal of most classroom education. Yet true creativity can be a messy process, and it produces multiple possible answers.

Applicants for employment with your organization have completed years of formal education, enough to stamp out whatever creativity they started life with. In fact, the more successful that employees were in school, the *less* creative they are likely to be. Success in school is directly tied to the ability to learn the system, to be socialized to the norms of the system—to learn to prize finding the single right answer. Highly creative people tend to be those least likely to have been socialized by a formal educational system.

Perhaps you have seen the nine-dot problem with instructions to connect the nine dots with four straight lines without picking up the pen. If not, look at Figure 4-1 and try to solve the problem before reading any further.

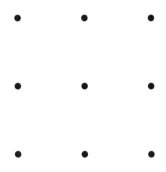

The task is to connect these nine dots using four straight lines without lifting your pen or pencil from the paper.

Figure 4-1. The Nine-Dot Problem

The reason most people have difficulty solving this problem is that they have been socialized to think within the rules. They even create their own rules or limits where none exist, as in this case. The secret is to go "outside" the nine dots before changing the direction of your line (see Figure 4-2). We often speak of going "outside the nine dots" in finding creative solutions to problems. Proactive futuring requires this kind of creativity and risk taking.

If the instructions had said, "Connect the nine dots with three lines" (or even two lines), a creative person could find the solution by pushing a little harder. If the instructions had said, "Connect them with one straight line," a creative person might realize the line could be any width. One swoop of a wide brush would connect all of them. Or perhaps the person would fold the paper so that one line would connect all of them. The secret of creativity is to push one step farther, then keep pushing and pushing.

High levels of creativity are critical if an organization is to be successful in a rapidly changing environment.

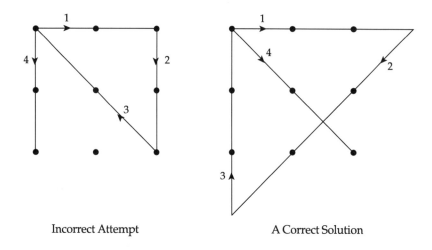

Incorrect Attempt   A Correct Solution

Figure 4-2. Solving the Nine-Dot Problem

Organizations can use numerous ways to increase their creativity level, including recruitment and selection methods, training techniques, job redefinition and redesign, changes in the reward system, removal of blockages, and use of tools to enhance creativity.

An organization can increase its level of creativity by deliberately recruiting for this important talent. Interviewing for creative behavior can be as important as interviewing for job skills. Asking for examples of the applicant's success in creative problem solving on the job or at school is one way to begin the process.

People can be trained to be more creative. Courses are available, and there are external consultants who specialize in delivering programs to enhance organizational creativity, especially the generation of creative ideas. Most people can dramatically increase their production of new and useful ideas in response to a given challenge. It is a matter of learning or relearning the necessary processes and enhancing or augmenting their natural creativity with specific techniques.

Organizations can also enhance creativity by redefining jobs, including making employees responsible for constantly improving the quality of their work. Another tactic is to give employees more responsibility for the work they perform, especially if it is accompanied by a removal of external controls. As organizations move the responsibility for quality from quality-control inspectors to the entire organization, the employees' conceptual approach to their jobs shifts dramatically; they see quality as their responsibility and act accordingly. A similar shift can occur when organizations expect employees to be creative and to generate new ideas.

At Toyota, clearly a world leader in improving creativity in the workplace, 93 percent of the employees are involved in submitting ideas each year. The average number of ideas submitted per employee is 47.6! Over 80 percent of those submitted are implemented—a far cry from the suggestion box found in most Western organizations—the one that is typically stuffed with discarded candy wrappers and other debris.

Toyota managers use a simple tool to obtain these suggestions: They ask employees how they would change their jobs in order to make it easier for them to perform—an attractive alternative for most people. However, Toyota employees know that management takes their ideas seriously and that good ideas have a strong chance of being implemented. This is in stark contrast to many U.S. automotive workers, who told us that their most common advice from managers was to "check their brains at the door"—even after working at a company for decades. What a high price to pay for this attitude! Loss of sales and increased competition have forced American automotive manufacturers to revise their management practices.

Job redesign can also enhance creativity. The more narrow the job, the less likely workers are to be highly creative about the work involved. Having a context for a task—and understanding how it fits into the flow of work—significantly increases the likelihood of generating ideas about how to improve the work done in that job. Redesigning jobs to broaden the range of tasks, including moving to teamwork, greatly increases the possibility of developing creative alternatives.

The truism in organizations is that you get what you reward, an important consideration in thinking about increasing creativity. If you reward quiet compliance, that is what you ordinarily will get. Witness the behavior of children in most classroom settings. If, on the other hand, you begin to reward creativity, you will greatly increase the rate of idea generation.

To increase creativity, it often is necessary to remove the organizational barriers to such creativity. These blockages include highly structured communication vehicles, restrictive supervisors, limited access to information, and restrictions on who can identify and solve problems. The concept of an organization involves the notion of "functional differentiation," the setting of boundaries and restrictions. Removing such boundaries can greatly increase the likelihood of generating creative ideas. Often the people who are at some distance from a given problem can generate the most useful ideas for solving it—even if it is a problem for which they have "no business" becoming involved.

Hewlett-Packard, one of the world's most innovative organizations, allows its employees relatively free access to electronic components in order to encourage them to be creative with them. This decision, which would be regarded as highly risky in most organizations, has resulted in the creation of many innovative products that might otherwise never have been conceived. Look for barriers to creativity and then get rid of them!

Increasing creativity may also require tools that foster this effort. Several personal-computer programs that enhance creativity are available. A number of books and self-development programs can also help. Making such tools available to all your employees can have a dramatic effect on them and can increase the overall creativity of your organization.

Innovation

Creativity alone is not enough; innovation is also necessary. Creativity is the generation of new ideas. Innovation is the application of these ideas in the real world. Moving from creativity to innovation is another of those changes that must be understood and carefully managed.

In implementing a strategic plan, it is always critical for the organization to make changes, to refocus itself, to develop a clearer sense of direction—in other words, to be innovative and not merely creative. Often the most necessary innovation required for an organization to reach its desired future is transformational organizational change, improvement, or renewal. We have seen how this was true in the case of British Airways.

Some organizations whose circumstances demand innovation do not, in fact, have any shortage of creative ideas, but they lack the will, desire, and experience to put these ideas into practice.

Like the family in the parable of turkey tails, organizations have traditions, well-established patterns of doing things the way they have previously been done. The older an organization is, the more established the traditions tend to be, especially if the predominant culture is role-oriented (Harrison and Stokes, 1992). All cultures rely on tradition to solve problems; after all, that is how cultures are typically defined. However, role-oriented cultures tend to rely on tradition more strongly and are less likely to question why turkey tails need removing. The Applied Strategic Planning process (see Chapter 5) forces organizations to ask the critically important question of why they are cutting off the turkey tail, and it allows for the possibility of leaving the tail on the turkey.

In most organizations new ideas do not find an easy home, especially if the ideas are generated elsewhere, by someone else's creativity. But the real question is what an organization can do when it understands that transforming a vision into reality requires innovations and changes that challenge traditional organizational wisdom.

Many organizations, in their growth and development, have inadvertently created organizational cultures that become relatively impervious to change. They stay frozen for long periods of time. In such a state, organizations are unready for change and can hold off virtually any visions of the future or new ideas for long periods. Visions and ideas, however, are a fragile commodity with a short shelf life.

Nurturing Ideas

A visionary frequently believes that the vision is so intrinsically attractive that it will sell itself without any marketing or other effort. This is almost never the case; most ideas die a premature death, because those who are needed to implement the vision do not understand it, do not identify with it, are content with the present state, or are too busy to pay attention to it.

A new idea can be compared with a newborn child. Human offspring require years of feeding, clothing, supporting, educating, training, and otherwise nurturing. A newborn colt, on the other hand, is on its feet within minutes after birth and is relatively self-sufficient within days. Many people who generate notions of change unfortunately see their ideas as self-sufficient young horses, not as dependent babies. Yet most such ideas require the same level of nurturing as human offspring do. The result is that many of these ideas, without sufficient support, nurturing, guidance, and fine-tuning, are never successfully sold into the organization. Thus, nothing happens. The desired future state is never reached.

The most prevalent way to try to increase innovation in an organization is by developing a separate research and development (R&D) group—a collection of creative folks who are freed of other responsibilities and charged with producing innovations.

Unfortunately, however, these R&D departments become too much like the rest of the organization. There is great pressure on R&D departments to produce. The R&D function in large organizations is often highly visible. This high visibility plus the great amount of pressure result in a strong fear of failure. This fear, in turn, quickly develops into a perceived need for careful documentation, testing, and retesting of each idea prior to a proposal that the new product or service become an organizational innovation.

In fact, this pressure has caused the R&D department in many organizations to be the *least* likely place to find effective innovations. When an effective innovation does come from the R&D department, it does so—in many cases—much later than is necessary, because of the continual testing and retesting. New products frequently emerge from an R&D lab well beyond the optimal time for successful introduction to the marketplace.

A classic story that illustrates the problems of R&D groups involves the Lipton Soup Company. Some years ago, Lipton's management decided to compete more directly with Campbell's Soup. The problem—as the Lipton managers saw it—was that Lipton's dry soups took ten minutes to prepare—from the point of opening the package to the point of consumption—whereas Campbell's canned soups took only three minutes. Therefore, Lipton's R&D people were asked to develop a "three-minute" soup, which would enable Lipton to effectively compete with Campbell's on the time dimension.

Months passed and still no three-minute soup. Under questioning by one of the executives about the team's continued failure, one of the R&D staff mentioned that they had produced an instant (under three minutes) soup but were still unable to come up with the specified product. Since the mandate had been to produce a "three-minute" product, they had rejected the instant soup as a failure.

Fortunately for Lipton, someone else was able to see the value in the rejected instant soup, which became an innovation that Lipton successfully carried to market. This story speaks directly to the difficulty experienced when organizations attempt to formalize innovation—when they understand the words but not the music.

Innovation in organizations can be dramatically increased by appropriate organizational structures and programs. One of the more successful programs used to encourage and support internal innovation in a major corporation is found at Kodak. The mission of its Office of Innovation is to significantly increase the number of internally generated creative ideas that become innovations.

An employee who has an idea that could become an innovation has a friend in the Office of Innovation.

The role of that office is not to carry ideas forward for employees but rather to help employees learn how to promote their own ideas in the corporation. This stance serves more than one purpose. First, the idea has a better chance of becoming an innovation if the parent of the idea stays with it, nurtures it, and tries to sell it. Second, the Office of Innovation—through coaching, problem solving, and resource-identification efforts—helps create idea champions.

Other Innovation Enhancements

Organizations have enhanced innovation in other ways. The 3M Company, for example, *requires* innovation by insisting that 25 percent of the sales in every product portfolio represent products that are less than five years old. Insisting on always having new products coming on stream is seen as the best way of avoiding technological obsolescence.

The 3M policy makes being innovative the norm, and this norm has been institutionalized. Such foresightedness is rare in organizations, and tradition still insists that turkey tails be removed. This is a risky position in our boiling-water environment.

One of the challenges to organizational leaders is to encourage innovation and risk taking that will effectively shape the organization's own strategic success.

Innovation is not limited to any single sector of the economy. In fact, an organization as unlikely as the Milwaukee Sewerage Commission has demonstrated high levels of innovation in tackling its work. In a state that generally has low levels of new business start-ups, the Milwaukee Commission has become one of the few sewage-treatment operations in the Western world to have figured out how to sell its processed sewage to the rest of the country! In fact, Milorganite, the lawn fertilizer produced by the Commission, has become a commercial success that has helped significantly offset the charges for sewage treatment to those served by the Commission.

Like other innovative organizations, the Milwaukee Sewerage Commission does not limit its innovative activity to simply having a product to sell. It has a marketing director and a strategic plan to link labor reductions with its retraining program to prevent workers from losing their jobs. One of its recent strategic concerns was what would happen if a brewery in the city would shut down and quit feeding mash into the sewer system. Such a change would lower the quality of the Milorganite and could negatively affect sales. To help avoid this reversal, plans were created to support the existing breweries in the city.

The Milwaukee Sewerage Commission is said to be the only major utility in the United States with a current building project that is both on schedule and under budget. It is currently charted to save the system $300 million in construction costs. This shows the impact that innovation can have on a service-oriented, not-for-profit organization.

Most organizations are finding themselves in what Lewin (1975) would regard as an unfreezing or unfrozen stage of existence. They have become unfrozen by their rapidly changing business and organizational environments. They are finding radically changing markets, heightened competition, more-demanding customers, and expectations of higher-quality products and services.

Furthermore, not-for-profit organizations are being challenged by for-profit organizations, and manufacturing firms are encountering international competitors that provide difficult-to-meet challenges. Even those institutions that historically have been solid and free from competition (such as hospitals, schools, or libraries) are finding competitors that threaten their once-secure lifestyle.

Innovation is the only way to successfully meet these challenges. Maintaining the present course of action is a prescription for disaster for most organizations—the path of the dodo bird. Innovation is critical to securing strategic success in today's turbulent times. Cutting off turkey tails can no longer go unquestioned.

The Role of Futurists

If tradition provides little or no solution to understanding today's problems, where then should managers turn for advice and help about the shape of things to come? After all, if they know how things will be, they can do a much better job of getting ready for the expected changes. As noted before, Ackoff (1981) terms such behavior *preactive planning,* or preparing for the future.

One resource to which managers can turn in such planning is futurists—those putative experts who suggest that their information about the future will help managers plan better. In fact, "futurism" has become a significant consulting specialty as organizations attempt to understand significant trends within the economy, within various demographic groupings, within various market segments, and so on, that directly affect them.

The future success or failure of many organizations hangs on the accuracy of experts' predictions about trends. The willingness of thousands of organizations to subscribe to newsletters, to hire consultants, and to otherwise try to find some certainty about the future in order to make appropriate decisions illustrates the breadth of this preoccupation. Managers, of course, should have the best information available as they guide their organizations into the future. However, no one can fully predict the trends and patterns of even a limited economic sector or marketplace with sufficient accuracy to assure the correct path for management decisions.

Failure to accurately predict the future was an important factor in the demise of Eastern Airlines. During a period of severe fuel shortages and high fuel costs, Eastern committed itself to a massive replacement of its fuel-inefficient airliners with highly fuel-efficient ones. The company based that decision on the advice of outside experts who believed the high fuel costs would be a long-term condition. This extensive program, which significantly extended the debt load of Eastern in order to accomplish the long-term goal of being a highly competitive airline, put Eastern at great risk and was the single most important reason for its final bankruptcy.

The assumption on which Eastern's critically important decision was made did not hold true. As fuel prices declined and fuel efficiency became less of a significant variable, the interest expense of financing the new airliners was no longer justified. Debt repayment became more difficult, and Eastern became less competitive than some airlines that had chosen to take a less-aggressive approach in updating their fleets. Thus, while it is prudent to attend to indicators about the future, there is also a risk in being guided solely by such indicators.

As organizations attempt to study and anticipate those forces that will be important in their future, "paralysis by analysis" is a real danger. The data on future trends are inconsistent and contradictory. There is always room for one more analysis or one more study before we make a decision. How we should move ahead is not always clear. What to do? The truly successful organizations—in the long run—make use of available information, recognizing it limitations, to establish the most likely success scenario and also actively attempt to shape their own destinies.

Proactive Futuring

If neither tradition nor the futurists provide definitive answers to planning for the future, what alternative is there? Again we recommend *proactive futuring*, wherein the organization decides what it wants the future to be and then moves toward making that vision a reality.

John Sculley, CEO of Apple Computer, provides a real-life example of the role of innovation in shaping strategic success through proactive futuring (Sculley and Byrne, 1987). Inventing Apple's future required the direct, active, creative application of a vision of the future and rested heavily on innovation and flexibility.

Early in its history, senior management at Apple decided that the sales of computers were limited by the difficulty of their use. They decided that they'd either have to open several hundred schools to teach people how to use their complicated computer—or develop a computer smart enough itself to make it easy to use. They bet the company on their belief that they could create such a computer. The Macintosh was the result—a machine that not only shaped Apple's future, but the whole world of micro-computers.

Proactive futuring is innovation of the highest order. Transforming a vision into reality involves the highest levels of creativity the organization can muster, competent planning, and a high degree of flexibility.

Flexibility

An increasingly important theme for long-term organizational success is developing and maintaining flexibility, especially the flexibility that supports innovation and change. In a constantly and sometimes radically changing business environment, such flexibility in responding becomes crucial. Given the inability to predict all the events that can require changes in a plan, it becomes important for organizations to develop strategies that allow significant timely readjustment if key variables change.

American Airlines's load-management process was an example of marketplace flexibility before the recent round of "fare simplification." The overall goal of the program was to fill as many seats as possible at the highest possible fare. Given the rich mix of coach-class fares, this was not an easy task. Nevertheless, it was better to fill the seats at a significant discount than not at all. American Airlines assigned a load manager to each flight to continually juggle the number of seats available in each price category to maximize revenues. Thus, the number of seats available at the lowest price would be small early on and, depending on the load factor, might increase before the flight date.

The load managers had a great deal of historical information on each of the flights assigned to them—how loads varied on different days of the week, in seasons of the year, on holidays, and so on. They based their allocations on these data, and they had the authority to continually make changes in those patterns. This method helps explain why you might not have been able to get a discount ticket a month before a trip but could during the week preceding the trip. American's load managers, who are not very high in the airline hierarchy, were empowered to make those decisions without any additional authorization. Empowerment in this case supported flexibility.

The County of Los Angeles Public Library provides an example of marketplace flexibility from the not-for-profit world. The largest circulating library in the United States, this system is currently confronting a dramatic increase in customer base—a 24 percent increase in the next twelve years. The traditional response in the library world would be a massive building program. The Los Angeles County system, however, has decided that the expense of building, maintaining, heating, and cooling libraries would be a major encumbrance on its ability to be flexible in meeting the real needs of its customers. Another consideration is that, once built, it is almost impossible to close a library facility, and that limits the library's options.

Alternative Plans

Given the changing demographics of Los Angeles County, building such monuments for books and other archival materials did not seem to be a reasonable option. An alternative that was finally included in the strategic plan for the County of Los Angeles Public Library was to develop a wide variety of service and product-delivery systems to supplement the traditional library facility. By providing books in kiosks, in leased space in shopping malls, and through home delivery, a library has more ability to shift resources as the population and the needs of library customers shift. Strategic plans need to enable organizations to have this level of flexibility to adjust to constantly changing market situations.

Key 8
Monitor and Manage "Down Board"

A significant aspect of successful flexibility is applying *down-board thinking*, which is how world-class chess players think. They must not only decide on their immediate moves, but they must look "down board" and consider their opponents' possible responses to their moves and plan a number of alternative moves ahead. Rather than thinking, "What is the best move I can make right now?" the player must consider the alternatives that each possible move would open to the opponent. The modern manager in an organization must become this type of player and consider how the competition would respond to the organization's plans.

Stories are legion about organizations that made good decisions for solving current problems but inadvertently caused themselves new and even larger problems by not thinking through the potential implications of their initial solutions—by not thinking down board. One example is the DuPont Chemical Corporation's plan to reduce its work force. It developed an effective plan to encourage employees to retire early by offering incentives that enabled them to do so. Unfortunately, the strategy was *too* effective. The plan was so enticing that many people who were needed for long-term viability of the organization took advantage of it. Thus, an extremely well-conceptualized plan to reduce expenses put the very future of the organization at risk. A simple dry-run of the plan would have revealed that it was simply too attractive.

Another example is found in the history of a now-defunct airline, People's Express. As a new type of airline, People's was a great success. It identified a market segment that was not well served—young and retired people for whom fares were the critical factor—and served them well. It selected and motivated a young work force that took an ownership role—both financially and psychologically—in the future success of the company. It became the sweetheart of the business press, apparently destined for even more success.

However, as it sought a way to grow out of the market niche in which it was successful into being a major carrier, it made a number of moves that had short-term payoffs but a significant negative impact on the viability of the company. The company's acquisition of Frontier Airlines created enormous internal operational problems, which in turn caused People's Express to lose customers and necessary profitability. Moves to better organize the growing company alienated the previously highly motivated work force and caused significant internal human resource problems. The net result of short-term moves to feed the growth strategy destroyed the viability of the airline and made it an easy acquisition target.

Down-board thinking is particularly relevant both in establishing a strategy (deciding what it is that we want to be) and in managing and monitoring the implementation of that strategy. In an organization that has developed a vision for itself—that has established a clear picture of its desired future—devising ways of making that vision a reality becomes critical. One of the keys to actually shaping that future is continually managing and monitoring the implementation strategy. Much like a missile, a strategy—once launched—must be carefully guided to its target. That guidance requires constant monitoring of its progress toward the target. Down-board thinking needs to be involved in this managing and monitoring function.

A Clear Picture of the Desired Future

Implementing the strategic plan—managing the tactics to ensure that the target will be reached—is critical to achieving strategic success. We believe that a B-quality plan with an A-quality implementation will outperform an A-quality plan with a B-quality implementation, because the implementation of a strategic plan is what will ultimately determine whether that plan will succeed.

Managing the plan requires developing detailed, well-reasoned tactics. It is not enough to have a clear vision of the Promised Land. We must have comprehensive and detailed tactical plans to get us from here to there. Without maps, compasses, transportation, provisions, clothing, tents, and the like, it is unlikely that we will ever arrive safely.

As each element of the tactical or implementation plan becomes clear, the other elements must be reviewed for congruity. For example, we may know how many camels we need to carry the pilgrims, but how many we will need for the provisions and other items will depend on the bulk and weight of those items. Thus, tactical plans need careful development and continual checking.

Monitoring involves the constant tracking of where the strategy is as it approaches the target. Monitoring the plan is facilitated if high-quality information systems are available. However, a second issue that must be confronted is the organization's willingness to adjust, fine-tune, and modify the strategy as required by the constantly changing marketplace.

Here is where strategic plans often break down; the planners persist, even when they have clear data that the plan requires modification. This was true in the case of Eastern Airlines—mentioned earlier—when clear-cut signs revealed that the oil crisis was receding. Yet Eastern was not willing to abandon its plan, once it was set into motion.

Not only does lack of willingness to modify a plan in action create the conditions for failure, but often organizations do not have adequately detailed implementation plans that allow for constant, close monitoring.

Typical issues that require monitoring include the following:

1. If this is the third quarter of the year, are we where we should be in the third quarter?

2. If this is year one of a five-year plan, are we where we should be at the end of year one?

The answers to such questions are critical. Systems need to be established that provide feedback on progress often enough to allow a redirection of the strategy or, at least, a reallocation of resources when the answers to such questions are negative.

Feedback loops must be regular and relatively frequent. Some organizations have only annual feedback loops. This is like navigating a ship in the middle of the ocean with only the rising and setting of the sun as guides. Gross measures alone are inadequate for monitoring strategic success. The quality of both the implementation plan and its monitoring methods is crucial to the eventual success of any strategic planning process.

Down-board thinking is critical not only in the strategic arena but in making daily management decisions. Each decision must be made with both a short-term and a long-term view. Each manager of an organization must constantly do a balancing act while asking, "What's the best solution to the problem that I am facing today, and how will that affect our strategic directions?" or "If we do this to solve today's problem, will it create new problems for tomorrow?" Down-board thinking about how the competition will react to a particular move should become a constant way of life in carefully monitoring and managing the organization's strategic directions.

Key 9
Maintain a Market Focus

The ninth key to successfully shaping your organization's future is maintaining a constant market-relevant focus. As important as the first eight keys are, they become irrelevant if customers do not want your product, if clients do not want your service, or if potential buyers do not choose to buy.

Although this statement may seem unbelievably basic, organization after organization—large, small, private, public, and so on—is finding itself out of touch with its customers. In the 1970s most organizations focused primarily on their own internal needs and only modestly on the needs of customers. The decade of the Eighties saw a sharp and significant increase in competitive pressures on organizations. This competition has led to the demise of many corporations and the retrenchment of some that were once thought to be invulnerable. However, it has also resulted—in the 1990s—in a focus on two elements:

1. How the organization can meet the needs of its markets.

2. How the organization can be effective in providing needed goods and services at a price that enables the organization to both grow and be profitable.

The organization that is intent on shaping its strategic success will not only learn to respond to the needs of the marketplace but will actively attempt to shape itself to meet the needs of its customers better.

There are already significant shifts in this direction among the more successful organizations. For example, organizations that previously viewed their customers as "clients" or "patients" or "patrons" are now seeing them as customers who have the ability to purchase services elsewhere. This shift toward meeting customer needs and wants can dramatically change the way in which business is done, the way organizations move into the marketplace, and ultimately the ways in which organizations succeed.

An increasing number of organizations have sought to identify ways of becoming more market aware and market driven. A great deal of attention has been paid to the handful of organizations that have historically been successful in maintaining a market focus. Organizations that have really succeeded in serving customers have thought of themselves as having an upside-down organizational chart. In these service-oriented, market-driven companies, the CEO, president, or executive director does not sit at the top of the pyramid, supported by all the other employees. Instead, the top of the organizational chart is occupied by the many people who have direct customer contact. Underneath are all the others—the CEO at the very bottom—who give support to those important customer-contact people, those who ultimately determine the success or failure of the organization.

In many organizations the need to shift toward a service-oriented structure is a difficult message to communicate, much less to sell. It is, nevertheless, a lesson that will be increasingly driven home by the marketplace itself.

To be successfully market driven, you must understand your customers in some depth. You must stop thinking about customers in terms of large numbers of homogeneous consumers of your products and services. The heterogeneity of today's marketplace makes that approach inappropriate and dangerous. To be truly market driven, *every* organization must become a niche marketer.

Traditional marketing literature tends to promote a mass-marketing mind-set, with niche marketing reserved for those boutique marketers who are not big enough or strong enough to compete with the grownups. This notion has proven to be dangerous.

Rapid change in thought and action is evident in even the largest organizations as they seek to create products and services tailored to the needs and wants of specific sets of customers. Kraft Foods, for example, under the ownership of Phillip Morris, developed an extensive campaign to extend its several product lines to entice new customers and appeal to niche markets. For example, Miracle Whip—a salad dressing and condiment—now comes in its traditional form for those who still want it, as Miracle Whip Lite for the calorie conscious, and as Miracle Whip Cholesterol Free for those who must restrict their fat intake.

A market-driven, niche-focused organization, which we believe all organizations must become, is a data-hungry organization. The commitment to becoming a niche marketer, or more likely a marketer to a mix of niches, involves constantly collecting information on the wants of the targeted customers. The focus must be on their "wants" and not their "needs." "Wants" are what lead to a positive decision to use the product or service, while "needs" are often attributed to the potential customer by someone else. Unless you turn these needs into wants, they are unlikely to lead to the buying decision that is necessary to your success.

If you are to meet the buyers' wants, you must study them carefully. This point is so important that Linneman and Stanton (1991) created an "ABCD of niche marketing—**A**lways **B**e **C**ollecting **D**ata." Information cannot be collected infrequently and episodically. Data collection must be constant and complete.

Clear avenues for the interpretation and dissemination of these data are also critical. The reason that some marketers succeed and others fail is that the successful ones constantly gather data, interpret that data, and then act on that information—all in a timely manner. This is true customer responsiveness. This strategy is especially critical in a niche-marketing world, because the smaller, more precisely defined niche can quickly change and could leave the unresponsive supplier out in the cold.

Those who adjust their thought patterns to this new reality, who develop market tracking systems, and who conceive products and services based on genuine customer wants will succeed. Those who fail to make such an adjustment will not. Customers are increasingly demanding high levels of quality and service.

In the 1990s almost no organization will serve as the customer's only option, and the customer will shape the market and determine who succeeds and who fails.

5

APPLIED STRATEGIC PLANNING

U sing the first nine keys for shaping a successful future for your organization may seem like a tall order, and it is. At times, you might have felt that we selected these nine keys randomly and that they bore no particular order or relationship to one another. However, the tenth key is really a master key for integrating the other nine. That master key is Applied Strategic Planning. Conducting Applied Strategic Planning for your organization is the one method for simultaneously applying the other nine keys in a way that will assure a bright future. What enables us to make such a claim? This chapter provides the answer.

Key 10
Conduct Applied Strategic Planning

Any organization embarking on strategic planning must face a number of important questions: What business is our organization really in? What business should it be in? How does the organization intend to achieve its long-term objectives? How much commitment to achieving these objectives do our mid-level managers have? How much commitment to these objectives do the rank-and-file employees have? How credible is our top-management team?

If neither you nor your organization can provide prompt, positive answers to these and myriad additional questions of equal impact and complexity, your strategic planning process is deficient or nonfunctional. You clearly are not using enough of the first nine keys to shaping your organization's future.

Most organizations do some kind of long-range or strategic planning, and the formal strategic planning process has been available for over fifty years. However, most strategic planning processes are poorly conceptualized and even more poorly executed. As a consequence, the resulting strategic plan rarely influences many of the daily decisions and specific activities of organizational members. All too often, strategic planning is seen as a top-management exercise that has little or nothing to do with the actual running of the business. In the hundreds of organizations with which we are familiar, strategic planning is often thought of as a document rather than a process. When completed, such documents are often simply filed away until a revision is again mandated—a sure prescription for becoming parboiled.

The Facilitator

What Is Strategic Planning?

We have a unique approach to defining strategic planning—one that requires an organization to do *proactive futuring* and enables it to avoid the boiled-frog syndrome.

We define strategic planning as "the process by which the guiding members of an organization *envision* the organization's future and *develop* the necessary procedures and operations to achieve that future." The vision of the future provides both a direction and the energy to move the organization in that direction.

Our definition of strategic planning focuses primarily on the *process* of planning, not the plan that is produced, although the final plan is of considerable importance. Successful strategic planning is characterized by organizational self-examination, confrontation of difficult choices, and setting of priorities.

Envisioning

This envisioning process, or proactive futuring, is very different from long-range planning. Long-range planning is a simple extrapolation of current business trends in an attempt to anticipate the future and prepare accordingly. Proactive futuring, however, involves a belief that the future can be influenced and changed by what we do now. Therefore, the model of strategic planning presented in this book helps an organization to understand that the strategic planning process does more than plan for the future: It helps an organization *create* its future.

The need for envisioning is vividly seen in the classic article "Marketing Myopia" by Theodore Levitt (1960). By *marketing myopia*, Levitt means a view of marketing that is limited to the goods or services a company provides. A broader view would include the customer's needs.

For example, Levitt contends that the failure of U.S. railroads to see themselves as being in the transportation business was the critical reason for their decline. The railroads declined not because the need for moving people and freight disappeared but because these needs were filled by other means—by airplanes, automobiles, trucks, and buses. Had the railroads defined their mission as transportation rather than "railroading," they might very well now have truck, airline, and bus divisions and still be a major industry. The only North American railroad that seems to have successfully understood and solved this problem is Canadian Pacific, which has developed into a total transportation company renamed CP Rail System.

Innovation

A major benefit of strategic planning is to help an organization see the big picture, especially from a marketing point of view (Key 9). Then the organization will be better able to understand the need for and to make the changes that are necessary in the new environment, rather than to continue to sit in the pan of boiling water and try inappropriately to adapt. These changes invariably will require Key 7 (encouraging innovation and flexibility).

An organization that constantly adapts to smaller changes in its industry may miss the fundamental shifts that can make the business obsolete. In recent years, many companies that manufacture personal computers or related products have been caught up in developing more and more powerful computers and equipment and have overlooked the fact that the market has become saturated. There is a limit to the number of such computers that can be absorbed by the market, and there is also a limit to the power that most buyers really need.

The reality of the market shift has caught many of these companies unaware, causing the need for extreme actions—such as extensive layoffs and major research-and-development cutbacks.

Goal Setting

Strategic planning is, however, more than just an envisioning process. It requires setting clear goals and objectives and attaining those goals and objectives during specified periods in order to reach the planned future state. Targets must be realistic, objective, and attainable.

The strategic plan of the Marriott organization to become the market leader in the hospitality industry is a case in point. In addition to undertaking large-scale expansion of its existing hotel chain in primary urban centers—such as New York's Times Square and Warsaw, Poland—and at major airports, Marriott purchased Host International (a nationwide chain of airport coffee and gift shops and airline catering) and a cruise-ship organization. It further segmented its hotel business by creating Marriott Courtyards (for a somewhat less "pricey" segment of the market at interstate-highway interchanges), Fairfield Inns (an even more down-market motel chain), and Residence Inns (for longer visits).

Marriott then began to enter the time-share condominium market with properties on Hilton Head Island, South Carolina, and in Tampa, Florida. In June 1986, it acquired Saga, the number-one institutional food service in the United States. Another major thrust has been to expand into retirement homes through its life-care system.

However, to its dismay, Marriott learned that airline catering and cruise ships are in different segments of the hospitality industry and no synergy occurred between these businesses and Marriott's major lines of activity. This, plus a need for cash during the recession of the late 1980s, led Marriott to divest itself of both of these businesses.

In its attempt to define its business, Marriott has continued to try a variety of new tactics and to quickly abandon those that do not work out, while maintaining its central, market-focused mission. This analysis supports the importance of continually using Key 9—maintain a market focus.

An Iterative Process

Strategic planning is an iterative process that must be repeated annually. Followed properly, it will lead to effective, strategic management that will influence the future of the organization. Strategic planning and strategic management (the day-to-day implementation of the strategic plan) are the two most important, never-ending jobs of management, especially top management.

The goals and objectives developed within the strategic planning process should provide an organization with its core priorities and with a set of guidelines for virtually all day-to-day managerial decisions. Once a strategic planning cycle is completed, the task of management is to ensure that the plan is implemented and then to decide on when to begin the next planning cycle. The future, by definition, is always before us; thus, organizations must always be in the simultaneous processes of planning and implementing their plans.

Rather than focusing on producing a product (the "plan"), Applied Strategic Planning is a process that is intended to develop a learning organization (Key 6) as the planning team acquires the necessary skills to cope with an ever-changing environment in innovative and flexible ways (Key 7).

Down-Board Thinking

A necessary component of effective strategic planning is down-board thinking. As noted in Chapter 4, down-board thinking is the term world-class chess players use to describe their own thinking processes; that is, they must not only decide on their immediate moves but also look "down board" and consider their opponent's possible responses to their moves and plan a number of moves ahead. So it is with strategic planning: The planning team must look down board, consider the implications of its plans, and then base additional plans on those implications.

For example, in the airline industry each major player knows that if it lowers its prices, its competitors will quickly follow suit. For an airline to successfully use a price-cutting strategy, it must quickly make such a decision and implement it, before its competitors can get wind of its intention. It must prepare an advertising campaign, typically to be unveiled on a Friday when it will be difficult for the competition to develop a prompt response. Although similar price cuts will be made immediately in the computer-reservation systems of competitors, several days will elapse before their advertisements can be published. The initial price cutter will harvest the ticket sales of those travelers who make early decisions based on its advertisements without thinking to check out the competition.

However, the airline making the initial cuts must further think through and plan for additional actions that competitors might take. With this sort of down-board thinking, decisions about pricing could be made and implemented in a far less frantic fashion. Such down-board thinking is Key 8 to successfully shaping your organization's future.

There is another important element in strategic planning—the business cycle—that can be seen as a special case of down-board thinking. Figures 5-1 and 5-2 demonstrate the relationship between business cycles and a typical organization's expansion modes. When an organization is new, it will most probably be in a survival mode. As the

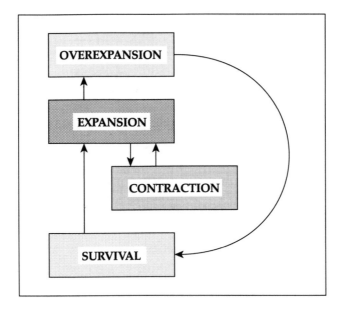

Figure 5-1. Expansion Modes

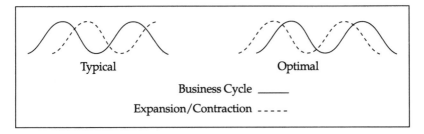

Figure 5-2. Business Cycles

organization experiences the business cycle rising, it typically starts expanding.

While the cycle is still high, when buying is costly and when good labor is scarce, the typical organization accelerates its expansion. As it sees the benefits of expansion, the organization can easily be trapped into thinking that if a little expansion is good, a lot of expansion is even better. And it continues to expand, even though the business cycle starts to decline. In fact, an organization typically will not start contracting until the business cycle has experienced significant contraction.

Often, the organization then discovers that it has money tied up in machinery and equipment that are lying idle. And too many people are on the payroll. Because the organization went into expansion at the wrong time or stayed in it too long, it has reached overexpansion and soon finds itself back in the survival mode. Extension of down-board thinking would eliminate, or at least sharply reduce, the problems caused by the mismatch of these two cycles.

An important goal in strategic planning is to keep within the expansion/contraction mode and to avoid the overexpansion and survival modes—to expand down-board thinking into managing business cycles. Let's look at how an organization can do this.

If a company begins to expand just as (or even better, just *before*) the business cycle begins to rise, it can buy at lower prices and will have a good selection of human resources. Then just before the cycle starts to fall, the company should start the contraction process. It should stay in the contraction mode until just before the business cycle begins to increase again. Thus, it would continually be moving from expansion to contraction to expansion but avoiding the overexpansion and survival modes.

Strategic planning and down-board thinking make it extremely difficult to continue the overexpansion-overcontraction process. Such organizational learning (Key 6) is one of the clear advantages of the Applied Strategic Planning process.

A New Strategic Planning Approach

Based on our research and consulting experience with over one hundred organizations, we have developed an approach to strategic planning that builds on several existing models but differs in content, process, and emphasis—especially its emphasis on application and implementation. The strategic plan is implemented and applied not only after it is completed but at nearly every step of the planning process—hence the title "Applied" Strategic Planning.

The use of this approach to strategic planning will provide new direction and new energy to an organization. This planning process (see Figure 5-3) with its clarity and sharpness, harnesses energy that may currently be dissipated in the system, and it reenergizes many who may have abandoned hope in the organization.

This approach, although originally designed for medium-sized organizations, is applicable to large and small organizations—and also to new business start-ups. The Applied Strategic Planning model is also as useful to governmental agencies and not-for-profit organizations as it is to business and industrial organizations.

This chapter provides an overview of the details of our approach and shows how it integrates the other nine keys to successfully shaping your organization's future. A more detailed exposition of our approach can be found in *Applied Strategic Planning: A Comprehensive Guide* (Goodstein, Nolan, and Pfeiffer, 1992).

The Applied Strategic Planning approach consists of nine sequential phases, with two of these phases (performance audit and gap analysis) essentially two differentiated aspects of a single phase; this approach also includes two continuous functions (environmental monitoring and application considerations), that are involved in all of the sequential phases.

In our model of the Applied Strategic Planning process we place three of the sequential phases (values scan,

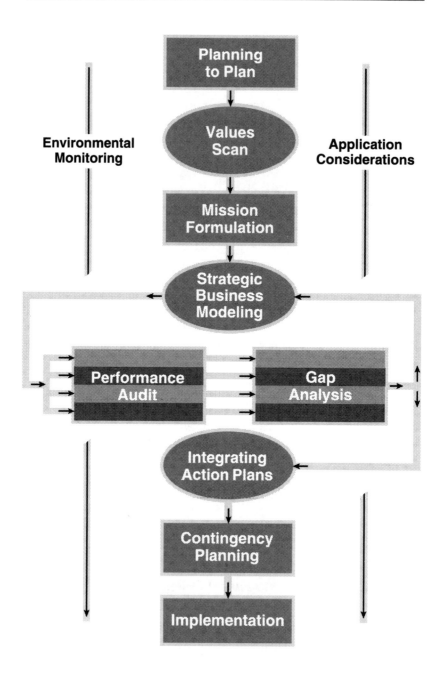

Figure 5-3. The Applied Strategic Planning Model

strategic business modeling, and integrating action plans) in ovals rather than rectangles to represent the unique elements of this approach. We emphasize them in this manner because we believe they are our model's "distinctive competency," an idea to which we will return later in this chapter.

Planning to Plan

The prework of the strategic planning process involves answering a host of questions and making a number of decisions, all of which are critically important to the eventual success or failure of the entire process. The following questions are typical of those that should be answered:

- How much commitment to the planning process is present, especially from the organization's chief executive officer?
- Who are the organization's principal stakeholders and how should they be involved?
- How do the organization's fiscal year and budgeting cycle fit the planning process?
- How long will the strategic planning process take?
- What information is needed in order to plan successfully?
- Who needs to gather and analyze the data?

The "planning to plan" phase requires finding answers to these questions before the actual planning sessions begin. Also prior to the planning sessions, the questions that people in the organization have about planning should be clarified, and the people who will be involved with the planning (i.e., the "planning team") should be identified. Obtaining organizational commitment from key players, especially the chief executive officer or executive director, is extremely important. Colin Marshall, CEO of British Airways, for example, chose to attend and "kick off" a series of management-training programs that were aimed at making British Airways "the world's favourite airline," an encapsulation of its strategic plan (Goodstein and Burke, 1991).

Usually it is necessary to engage an objective third party to facilitate the strategic planning process. This person can be from inside the organization (such as a human resources trainer or planner), but it is generally preferable to bring in someone from outside (a consultant) to maximize objectivity throughout the process.

Environmental Monitoring and Application Considerations

As noted earlier, Applied Strategic Planning involves both discrete and continuous elements. The continuous processes are *environmental monitoring* and *application considerations*; both are issues that need to be addressed immediately at whatever point they emerge in the deliberations of the planning team. We will consider these continuous elements briefly before returning to the discrete phases.

Environmental Monitoring

Environmental monitoring—perhaps more than any other factor—will help the frog to realize it must jump out of the pan. Throughout the planning activity, management needs to be aware of things that are happening inside and outside the organization that might affect it. In particular, there are five environments that need to be monitored: the macro environment, the industry environment, the competitive environment, the customer environment, and the organization's internal environment (see Figure 5-4). Naturally, some of these environments overlap one another.

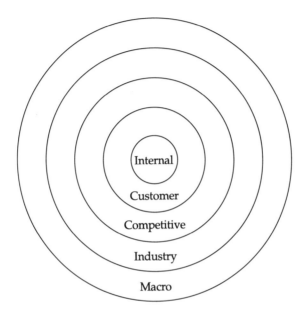

Figure 5-4. Environments to Be Monitored

The environmental monitoring process, which includes competitor analysis, should be continual, so that the appropriate information about what is happening or about to happen in the various environments is always available to the planning group. Strategic planning provides an opportunity to integrate much of the data the organization already collects. Environmental monitoring is the way organizations should collect, assess, and develop action plans for dealing with the information that the scout bees have brought back to the hive.

The Limited (a highly successful, growth-oriented retail giant) is well known for its unrelenting attention to environmental surveillance. It monitors, primarily through computer-generated information, the internal operations of the organization (sales, inventory, and out-of-stock items) and moves quickly to keep its many business elements in alignment. It regularly monitors its customers, and it also monitors the way it is perceived by fashion-conscious, trendy groups of buyers.

Equally regularly, it monitors its competitors and the world-wide fashion industry in order to purchase raw materials, choose styles, and establish production schedules. Leslie Wexner, CEO of The Limited, believes that this attention to detail is an important factor in the company's success. This example illustrates how the environmental monitoring phase of Applied Strategic Planning helps assure the use of Key 9—maintaining a market focus.

Application Considerations

Although implementation of the strategic plan is the final step of the model, there is a continual need to pay attention to action steps throughout the planning process, without waiting for implementation of the final plan. As an organization moves through the planning process, it needs to be aware of available resources, the existing culture, and what the competition is up to. Otherwise, the planning process becomes an academic exercise.

At each phase of Applied Strategic Planning, certain application considerations should be addressed rather than being postponed until the final implementation phase. Making such decisions and then executing them involves not only Key 5 (empowerment), but also Key 4: promote and reward risk taking.

Identifying a problem and then solving it always involves some risk. The Applied Strategic Planning process promotes such risk taking and also helps create or sustain an organizational reward system for supporting risk-taking behavior.

Environmental monitoring and attention to application considerations are also hallmarks of a learning organization. Both of these continuous processes develop an organizational mind-set that encourages members to attend to environmental feedback and then develop new and better ways of responding to that information. These processes turn the organization into one that is constantly attempting to learn how to do its job better—Key 6.

Values Scan

The values scan encompasses the values held by each member of the planning team and by the group as a whole, as well as those of stakeholders who will be affected by the

An Examination of Personal Values

strategic plan. The values scan includes an examination of the personal values of the members of the planning team and of the organization's current values, philosophy of operations, and culture. These steps require the organization to use Key 1: base decisions on values.

Early in the planning process, differences in the values of individual members of the planning team need to be identified, clarified, and (where possible) resolved. For example, if individuals' values such as security, risk taking, integrity, and openness are not explored and legitimized, it is unlikely that the organization's plan can truly reflect the desires and ambitions of the planning team.

If these values are not fully examined, the team may reach little or no agreement about how the organization's future will fit with the expectations of the key members of the management group. For example, a senior-management team that is consciously or unconsciously fixated on its own perks and retirement benefits is unlikely to adopt any strategy that puts these perks at risk. Once there is clarity and some agreement—or ideally a consensus—on values, the strategic planning process can move ahead; but this can be a difficult and time-consuming business.

Once the values of the planning team have been examined, the values of the organization as a whole need to be identified and explored. An organization's values are reflected in the way the organization approaches its work, sometimes explicitly articulated in the organization's published philosophy of operations.

One example of such a statement is the "Five Principles of Mars" (see Chapter 2). It briefly focuses on the importance of the values of quality, responsibility, mutuality, efficiency, and freedom in the operation of the business and its relation with customers, suppliers, and others.

This type of statement integrates the organization's values into the way the company does business. Organizations that have an explicit philosophy of operations can legitimately expect all employees to abide by the philosophy. True values are supported by rewards and sanctions. At M&M Mars, for example, any employee found violating one of the five principles is disciplined. Likewise, those found supporting or demonstrating adherence to these principles are likely to experience formal or informal rewards. The point is employees have clear guidelines.

Philosophy of Operations

All organizations have philosophies of operation, whether or not those philosophies are stated explicitly. If an organization has an implicit philosophy of operations, part of the strategic planning process is to make that philosophy explicit. The strategic plan must fit the philosophy, or the philosophy needs to be modified (a task that should only be undertaken with significant organizational support for the change).

Stakeholders

The values of the organization's other stakeholders also need to be considered as part of the scanning process. Stakeholders typically include the organization's owners or shareholders (or the funding agency of a not-for-profit or governmental organization), the employees (including all managers), customers, suppliers, unions, and governments.

Members of the community who believe that they have a stake in the organization, regardless of whether such a belief is accurate or reasonable, should not be ignored. The nuclear-power industry, for example, failed to recognize community groups and environmentalists as stakeholders ("What right do they have to dictate to us?"). Currently that industry has extensive problems, in part because it failed to cultivate a relationship with these external stakeholders.

Organizational Culture

The values scan also examines the organization's culture. As Chapter 2 pointed out, an organization's culture is rooted in its assumptions about the way things work. These assumptions in turn give rise to values, which in turn bring about organizational norms—"the way we do things around here."

It is important in examining an organization's culture to begin with a study of the assumptional base that lies at the root of the culture. This analysis is one of the most important and—at times—difficult activities of the planning process. It requires an in-depth examination of the fundamental beliefs that underlie organizational life and organizational decision making and how they have created both the organization's values and its norms.

Such explorations will almost inevitably lead to confrontations as planning-team members begin to clearly understand the nature and depth of the differences among them. These confrontations can be long and involved. Without such efforts, however, differences in assumptions, values, philosophy, and norms will continually surface in the planning process and block the group's progress.

Once the values are successfully clarified and resolved, at least to some extent, the differences are less likely to interfere with the planning process. Then it will be relatively easy to move into the next stage of the planning process and thus to base the organization's decisions on values (Key 1).

Mission Formulation

The planning team can next turn its attention to developing a mission statement. This should be a brief statement (one hundred words or less) that identifies the basic business the organization is in. The mission statement should be easily understood by and communicated to all members of the organization.

The New Mission

The mission formulation phase involves identifying clearly what business the organization wishes to be in (envisioning) and specifically stating it—Key 2. The vision of the future should energize and steer the members of the organization; that is, it should inspire a rallying cry (Key 3).

The mission statement should be a transformational guide to what management wants the organization to be. For example, when Robert Townsend, as the new CEO at

Avis (the car-rental company), asked management to examine its operations, he discovered that a significant portion of the company's business involved the sale of used rental cars. In fact, Avis was the world's second largest "producer" of used cars. As a result, the company's mission was altered to include a statement that the company would seek to provide the best used cars possible. Policies (about the type of cars that would be purchased and how they would be equipped) and daily practices (such as vehicle maintenance) soon changed to fall in line with the new goal. When employees viewed a rental car as a product for sale rather than a waste product, a different mindset quickly emerged.

In formulating its mission, an organization needs to answer four primary questions (see Figure 5-5):

1. *What* function does the organization serve?
2. For *whom* does the organization serve this function?
3. *How* does the organization go about filling this function?
4. *Why* does the organization exist? (What broad social need does it serve?)

What

Organizations need to answer the "what" question in terms of the customers' needs (or—as mentioned in Chapter 4—the customers' "wants") that the organization meets or attempts to meet. If an organization identifies itself as meeting certain public needs, it will have a clearer and more efficient charter for decisions and operations, making it less likely to experience obsolescence and decline—especially if its clients or funding sources share this belief.

For example, when a company that manufactured drill bits examined its mission from the standpoint of benefit to

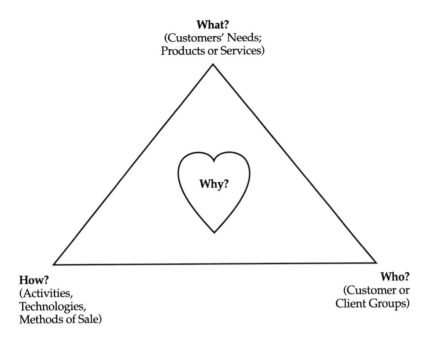

Figure 5-5. Four Basic Elements of the Organizational Mission

the customer, it came to the realization that it was actually in the business of helping customers to make holes, rather than producing drill bits. The company then began to develop products that involved the latest laser technology to improve its customers' ability to make holes.

If petroleum producers see themselves as being in the business of providing sources of energy to consumers, many new options open to them: geothermal, solar- and wind-power generators, and so on. The major issue in this facet of mission formulation is achieving consensus on how broadly or narrowly to answer the "what" question.

Who

Identifying the "for whom" is another concern of mission formulation. No organization, no matter how large, can meet all the needs of all its possible clients or customers. The mission formulation process requires a clear identification of what portion of the total potential customer base an organization considers as its primary market.

The process of sorting out the potential customer or client base and identifying which portion should be sought out by the organization is called *market segmentation.* Markets can be segmented in many ways: geographically, ethnically, financially, and so on. For example, needs of Sun Belt consumers are different from those of Frost Belt consumers; kosher foods have devoted consumers, as do soul foods; and Federal Express serves customers who are willing to spend more than the price of ordinary postage to ensure next-day delivery of packages.

How

If the planning team has identified what the organization does and for whom, it must now decide how the organization will proceed in achieving these targets. The "how" may involve a marketing strategy, such as being the low-cost producer, the technological leader, or the high-quality manufacturer. Or it may involve a distribution system (such as regional warehouses), evening classes that meet in offices or plants, transportation services for clients, or no-appointment medical treatment facilities in shopping centers. It may involve customer service, personalized selling, or any of a variety of processes through which an organization can deliver products or services to a defined consumer group.

Why

The question of "why" the organization exists—its *raison d'etre*—is critical to mission clarity. This existential question can be asked first, of course, but it *must* be asked, for both profit-making and not-for-profit organizations.

With the growing social consciousness of organizations in the Nineties, the why question can hardly go either unasked or unanswered. It thus appears as the "heart" in Figure 5-5. Developing clear answers to these four questions results in a crystal-clear mission statement (Key 2).

Distinctive Competency

Another important ingredient in the mission statement is identification of the organization's distinctive competency— that is, the quality or attribute that sets the organization apart from its competitors. In other words, what is the unique advantage that can be exploited? Identifying the organization's distinctive competency represents a special aspect of Key 9 (maintaining a market focus).

Drafting the Statement

Once all the elements have been identified, they can be woven into the organization's mission statement. The statement should be worded in a way that will provide a rallying cry to the organization (Key 3). Sometimes the planning team must persevere in crafting and recrafting the statement until it does serve as that rallying cry.

Drafts of both the mission statement and the philosophy of operations need to be distributed through the organization for review and comments. This review should not be a boring exercise; it should be a structured activity that encourages involvement and action. For instance, Johnson & Johnson annually takes a day for in-depth discussions of the company's Credo and how well it has been applied since the last such meeting. This involvement and commitment is an example of how Key 5 (empowerment) is used in the Applied Strategic Planning model.

Developing an effective mission statement can be a time-consuming task, but it must be completed before the planning team moves to the next step. The mission statement provides an enormously valuable management tool to an organization; it charts its future direction and establishes a basis for organizational decision making. Key 8 (down-board thinking) must be used in formulating the mission statement.

Strategic Business Modeling

Strategic business modeling is the process by which the organization specifically defines success in the context of the business(es) it wants to be in, how that success will be measured, what will be done to achieve it, and what kind of organizational culture is necessary to achieve it. This definition of success should be consistent with the newly established mission statement.

Strategic business modeling encompasses the organization's initial attempts to spell out in detail the paths by which the organization's mission is to be accomplished and how progress toward achieving that mission will be tracked. In short, strategic business modeling produces a concrete, detailed road map of the organization's desired future.

Proactive Futuring

The strategic business modeling phase is another excellent point for deciding not to adapt to the hot water. It requires the planning team to consider jumping out of the pan and creating a future.

In proactive futuring, the organization takes responsibility for its own future rather than waiting for external forces to dictate that future. In other words, proactive futuring requires the innovation and flexibility of Key 7. As mentioned in Chapter 3, Procter & Gamble's development of the disposable diaper is a good example of proactive futuring.

Strategic business modeling provides the planning team with the last opportunity to either develop or reshape its vision of an ideal future before getting down to the nuts and bolts of figuring out how to reach that future.

Constructing a Strategic Profile

Prior to getting down to the details, however, the planning team should construct a strategic profile on the organization. This is an attempt to identify the organization's general orientation or mind-set to strategy formulation. The strategic profile involves four elements:

1. The organization's approach to innovation (Key 7)
2. Its orientation to risk (Key 4)
3. Its capacity for proactive futuring (Key 9)
4. Its competitive stance (Key 8)

Each of these elements is important in setting the stage for selecting the pathways that will achieve the organization's mission.

The Process

The actual process of strategic business modeling consists of the following four major elements:

1. Identifying the major lines of business (LOBs) or programs that the organization will develop to achieve its mission.
2. Establishing the critical success indicators (CSIs) that the organization will use to track its progress in each of the LOBs it pursues.

3. Identifying the strategic thrusts that are required to allow the organization to achieve its mission. (Some examples of strategic thrusts are globalization, total quality management, and faster cycle time.)

4. Determining the culture necessary to support the LOBs, CSIs, and strategic thrusts.

Each of these four elements must be determined and independently worked through during the next two phases of Applied Strategic Planning (performance audit and gap analysis). After gap analysis it is sometimes necessary to loop back and revise the elements of the strategic business model before proceeding to the action plans. This possibility again illustrates the need for perseverance in the Applied Strategic Planning process.

The Performance Audit

The questions raised during the performance audit are easy to ask but hard—and sometimes painful—to answer. After envisioning the organization's future, checking out its strategic profile, and identifying LOBs, CSIs, strategic thrusts, and the culture necessary to achieve that future, the planning team must evaluate where the organization stands in each of these areas. The gap between the organization's current status and its desired future is the measure of how far it must travel to get where it wants to go.

Nevertheless, before the journey can be accurately planned, it is imperative that the planning team clearly understand the organization's present location. The performance audit is an organized, concerted effort to identify where the organization is today.

SWOT Analysis

SWOT (strengths, weaknesses, opportunities, threats) analysis is an in-depth, simultaneous study of the organization's current internal *strengths* and *weaknesses* and the external *opportunities* and *threats* confronting it. The SWOT analysis examines those factors both internal and external that may positively or negatively affect the organization's future.

The SWOT Analysis

The performance audit examines the recent performance of the organization on the same basic performance indices (production, quality, service, profit, return on investment, and cash flow) that have been identified as critical success indicators (CSIs). Any data that can help the organization better understand its present capabilities for doing its work should be included in the audit. Such data might cover life cycles of existing products, employee productivity, inventory turnover, facilities (including capacity and condition), and management capability.

In executing the performance audit, special attention should be paid to obtaining the hard data that indicate the organization's capacity to move in the identified strategic directions. Unfortunately, businesses do not always do this.

For example, in 1991, shortly before Christmas, General Motors announced a plan to reduce its work force by 74,000. For over a year GM had been losing over US$1.5 million *per day*, a fact well reported in the business press. Yet, despite the widespread knowledge of this fact, GM took no action to stop the fiscal hemorrhaging until its credit rating was threatened. A drop in its credit rating would have raised the cost of the money borrowed by GMAC, its finance subsidiary and its most profitable LOB. Even though this threat spurred the plans for a work-force reduction, there was no indication that GM was reconsidering its strategy or its strategic business model—the root causes of its problems.

Need for Candor

The need for candor, openness, and nondefensiveness during the performance audit cannot be overstated. Defensiveness leads to finger pointing, avoiding blame, and other trust-destroying behaviors. If such behaviors are allowed to dominate the audit process, they quickly hinder the planning efforts. Candor, openness, and nondefensiveness require risk taking (Key 4), one of the necessary ingredients of Applied Strategic Planning.

Gap Analysis

The gap analysis represents the "moment of truth," when the planning team must determine the size of the gap between the strategic business model and the organization's current performance.

Confronting this gap can perturb and dishearten even the most hardy members of the planning team as they confront the discrepancies between what is and what is hoped for. The planning team's task is to find ways to close each of the identified gaps.

If it is impossible to bridge a gap, the planning team must return to the strategic business model and rework it until the gap between the profile and the organization's capacity to achieve it is reduced to a manageable size. Therefore, the diagram of the Applied Strategic Planning process depicts not only arrows running forward from strategic business modeling to performance audit and then to gap analysis, but also an arrow running backward from gap analysis to strategic business modeling.

Closing the Gap

Examining where the organization is and comparing this picture with where it wants to be may require several iterations before all gaps can be closed. Occasionally the mission statement also has to be modified in the process.

A small electronics manufacturer with whom we consulted had to abandon its growth strategy when gap analysis revealed that its debt load was too high for the company to obtain the funds needed to reach the projected growth.

If gap analysis reveals a substantial disparity between the performance audit and the strategic profile or the strategies identified for achieving the profile, more major changes in the organization may be required. For example, the organization may be too centralized; it may need to be decentralized to obtain the desired levels of performance — a strategic thrust. Obviously, either the capability of the organization or the level of expectations of performance needs to be modified in order to close the gaps between the plan and the organization's capacity.

Gap analysis is another place in the Applied Strategic Planning process where candor—and risk taking (Key 4)—are necessary. It serves little purpose if the planning team deceives itself and the rest of the organization about how well positioned the company is to execute the strategic business model. An inappropriately optimistic analysis of the gap only postpones the real day of reckoning—when the organization's resources prove to be inadequate to close the gap.

Integrating Action Plans— Horizontally and Vertically

Once the strategy for closing the gaps has been developed and initiated, two important issues need to be addressed:

1. Each of the various constituent units of the organization—business (the vertical dimension) and functional (the horizontal dimension)—need to develop detailed operational or tactical plans based on the overall plan of the organization. Each of these plans should reflect the overall mission and should also involve budgets, marketing plans, and timetables.

2. Each of these unit plans needs to be integrated into a comprehensive plan.

Almost invariably, developing these unit plans makes it clear that the plan exceeds the resources of the organization—time, human, financial, production, marketing, and so on. The tough decisions then facing the organization involve how to set priorities—for example, which lines of business will receive more attention early and which can wait, or which strategies will be emphasized first and which will be placed "on hold" until additional resources are available. This integration is yet another example of how multiple keys to successfully shaping your organization's future are involved in every phase of Applied Strategic Planning.

Contingency Planning

The Applied Strategic Planning process appropriately focuses on the highest-probability events confronting the organization, especially those with high impact. But this focus would result in an incomplete set of plans, a problem solved by contingency planning.

Contingency planning focuses on those lower-probability events that would have a high impact on the organization if they were to occur. The most important contribution that contingency planning can make to an organization is the development of a *process* for identifying and responding to unanticipated or less likely events. Since it is impossible for any organization to identify and plan for all the lower-probability events that might have a significant impact on it, developing a way of tracking and responding to such events is generally the most functional approach.

In doing contingency planning, it is important not only to consider the potential threats that can develop, but also the opportunities.

Contingency planning provides the organization with alternative business-modeling strategies that can be used with a variety of scenarios. For example, producers of building materials are heavily influenced by new housing starts, which—in turn—are a function of interest rates and general economic conditions. In developing its strategic business model, a producer of building materials may identify several alternative futures, each based on a different volume of housing starts. Housing starts, in turn, are influenced by a variety of governmental actions. For example, if the U.S. tax laws were modified so that people could no longer take tax deductions for mortgage interest paid on their residences, housing starts would clearly be threatened. On the other hand, a large governmental program to subsidize residential construction would be an opportunity. Contingency plans should be developed on the basis of both kinds of alternatives, and contingency planning requires the constant use of down-board thinking (Key 8).

Implementation

Many strategic plans die before they are fully implemented. Careful attention to doing what has been planned is critical.

The real test of the final implementation of the strategic plan is the degree to which managers and other members of the organization use the strategic plan in their everyday decisions on the job. Ideally, the manager will pause to consider whether a proposed solution to a problem is congruent with the organization's strategic plan.

If Applied Strategic Planning has been properly done, the plan will be based on the organization's explicit values (Key 1), and the mission statement (Key 2) will provide a rallying cry around which the organization can persevere (Key 3). The plan will also promote and reward risk taking (Key 4), empower the people (Key 5), encourage the development of a learning organization (Key 6), and require innovation and flexible (Key 7) down-board thinking (Key 8) with a strong market focus (Key 9). If all of these keys have been used in the Applied Strategic Planning process, the task of implementation, while never without its obstacles, will be readily manageable.

In Conclusion

The acid test for any strategic planning process is the degree to which it affects the ongoing behavior of the organization. The strategic plan needs to become the template on which organizational decisions are based.

A complete Applied Strategic Planning process makes certain that each of the nine other keys to successfully shaping an organization's future has been properly used to unlock the full power of the organization. There are, of course, several other elements that are essential for ensuring a successful Applied Strategic Planning process. These include proper assumptions, a comprehensive environmental monitoring system, organizational competence—and just a little bit of luck!

Strategic planning can give leaders the ability to shape the future of their organization. Applied Strategic Planning offers the sense of control that is all but absent in many organizations. While there are many positive consequences, Applied Strategic Planning—properly done—offers the best insurance against becoming a boiled frog!

6

THE CHALLENGE

The challenge is yours. As you come to the conclusion of this book, you must determine whether you want to shape the future of your organization. Reviewing the ten keys, you must determine whether you are willing and able to use them to succeed. You must make a personal commitment to action, or no proactive organizational change will occur.

The Need to Shape the Future

You must determine the level of need within your organization to shape its future. The fact that you picked up this book and have read this far indicates some acknowledgment of need on your part.

Return for a moment to Chapter 1 and examine the results of the quick self-test (Figure 1-2). Most organizations today would discover that there is a significant "heating up of the water" surrounding it. For these organizations, shaping the future becomes imperative to future success and, in many cases, future existence. For these organizations—and for yours if you fit into this category—the question of "whether" to proceed with shaping the future is academic. The question is much more clearly *how* to proceed and *what* to push aside in order to acquire the resources necessary to succeed in the process of shaping the future.

If your organization has demonstrated that it is only in "warm water," you have a choice. You can decide to shape your future and proceed at a somewhat leisurely pace, or you may determine that—even though your organization does not appear to be in an immediately stressful situation—the water is rapidly heating up and you want to proceed more rapidly to avoid major disaster.

As you explore the need for your organization to shape its future, skim Chapter 1, review the environmental shifts and stresses that are outlined there, and answer the following questions:

1. Is the "bigger is better" trap an issue for your organization?
2. Has your organization grown too large to compete in rapidly changing markets?
3. Are the post-Cold War changes that are hitting so many aspects of the economy important to your future?
4. Are you affected by the changing international relationships that are taking place?
5. Do you have outdated organizational structures that inhibit your ability to succeed in the long term?
6. Have you resolved the need for faster cycle time?
7. Have you "solved" the quality issue within your organization?
8. Do you have current levels of quality at industry standards? Can you continue to improve these levels?

The answers you give to each of these questions will help determine your need to actively shape the future of your organization.

Continuing to examine the points in Chapter 1, determine if any of the blocks to shaping the future identified there are present in your organization. If so, they need to be dealt with. Your organization's ability to have a vital future pivots on not perpetuating these blocks to your own success. Realize that some of these blocks may be so deep, so troubling, or so anxiety-provoking for key members of the organization that members will have a strong tendency

The Challenge

to collude—to say to one another that "there really is no problem."

For example, if there is a tendency in your organization to avoid risk taking, members may believe this tendency is justified by their perceived lack of resources—or some other equally appealing argument. Nevertheless, for your organization to succeed in the long term, such blockages must be effectively removed. Their existence can indicate a need to take control of your organization's future. You must fight the tendency to avoid dealing with them.

Barriers to Successfully Shaping the Future

What are the barriers to successfully shaping the future of your organization? What could prevent you from succeeding in this crucial endeavor? Unfortunately, there are *many* barriers to succeeding at this process. First, examine the ten keys (Chapter 1). Failure to accomplish any one of them can seriously limit the potential of your organization. Failure of two or more makes it extremely unlikely that you will succeed at shaping your future. To develop a "formula for failure" or a list of barriers, imagine the reverse of each key. This formula for short fall, disappointment, and failure would look something like the following:

Formula for Failure

1. Base decisions on what works—not on what you believe. Do not base decisions on values.

2. Proceed with a fuzzy mission. Do not waste time developing a clear vision.

3. Plan on an easy, quick process. Do not develop followership.

4. Avoid risks and reward other members who successfully avoid taking them.

5. Encourage all members of the organization to feel helpless, unempowered, and unable to do anything about the organization's future.

6. Discard this foolishness about being a "learning" organization. It sounds like the mission of a school.

7. Carefully maintain the status quo. Firmly take your stand; be wary of innovations.

8. Focus on today. It is the only thing that really counts.

9. Focus internally. Above all, make sure operations are orderly.

10. Implementing a strategic plan is a futile exercise, especially in these periods of rapid change; so if the CEO insists on planning strategically, persuade him or her not to choose Applied Strategic Planning.

The Hierarchy

Although we were trying to be satirical—even ludicrous—when we created this list, we realized that it is all too true of many organizations. Although their leaders would never admit support of or adherence to this list, they regularly behave as though they have a master plan for failure.

There are additional barriers to successfully shaping the future of your organization. It is important for us to identify them here, because they can easily limit the success of your efforts. As this discussion proceeds, remember that these barriers are in addition to both those discussed in Chapter 1 and those in the above "formula for failure." They constitute elements that prevent an organization from using the ten keys to success.

Organizational Structures

In most organizations, organizational structures are a major barrier to shaping the future. The very act of organizing a company or a not-for-profit organization means the sorting out of resources and responsibilities. In most organizations this is translated to formal structures, often reflected by written organizational charts, formal recording and communication patterns, and clear delineation of responsibility along hierarchical patterns. These formal structures create barriers to success in shaping the future for two major reasons:

1. The formal structures work slowly and inefficiently or not at all, thus limiting the ability to create an effective vision for the future and develop the necessary followership to achieve that vision.

2. The current inhabitants of each box on the organizational chart have a "turf" orientation. The formalization of structure has created constituencies for the status quo.

The incumbent management and staff within any line of business, support group, or other organizational division will often spend inordinate energy protecting that line of business from careful analysis, phase out, and—sometimes—even the opportunity for growth! Therefore, the effort to successfully shape the future can easily be held hostage to current organization structures.

To be successful, the organization leadership will have to overcome the limits of current structures. As indicated in Key 7, it will also be imperative not to reestablish such deep and potentially unchangeable structures.

Paradigms

Current *mind-sets* or *paradigms* that shape thought within an organization or industry present another barrier to successfully shaping the future of the organization. Joel Barker, in his book *Future Edge* (1992) has become the national "poster person" for the paradigm issue. He contends that as people spend more and more time within a given industry producing products and services with which they become increasingly familiar, they develop deeper and deeper "ruts" regarding their work.

These patterns of behavior and thought—paradigms—have both an up side and a down side. The up side is that they effectively coordinate effort and reduce inefficiency. The down side is that they close off new ways of thinking about the work and therefore often reduce creativity and innovation. The current paradigms in your organization and your industry are likely the enemies of an effort to successfully shape the future, for they close off opportunity. People oftentimes cannot even see the possibilities the future holds because they are limited by seeing the world through glasses with lenses ground and shaped by the successes and failures of the past. Effectively managing these paradigms, which involves both maintaining those that are useful and breaking free from those that are limiting, is critical to your effort to shape the future of your organization.

A prevalent mind-set in many organizations supports the adage "If it ain't broke, don't fix it." Although this adage has been repeated so many times that it has become a cliché, it is a disastrous philosophy for running one's life or one's organization. If we wait until something is broken to begin the process of fixing it, we will likely be far too late to accomplish the repair. At the point that an organization is visibly broken, resources may be dissipated, time may have run out, markets may have been dominated by others, or other factors may have occurred that make successful shaping of the future extremely difficult if not impossible.

Lack of Resources

Lack of resources is often a barrier to successfully shaping an organization's future. Doing so calls for significant commitment of resources of all types—finances, people, facilities, and technology. These resources must be identified, committed, and employed in a timely fashion. Many organizations find themselves lacking in key resource areas. They have limited capital with which to finance their future or lack the key human resources necessary to conceive, design, and accomplish their ideal vision of the future. Some lack the physical facilities necessary to succeed, and others—in this technological age—fail to have the necessary technology. All these deficiencies become significant barriers to future success.

Financial Resources

Resource limitations may well be of the organization's own making. Failure to set aside financial resources to fund future success is a prevalent pattern in Western organizations of every type. This focus on the present, and the resulting lack of investment in the future, is often the result of a short-term mentality held by key internal and external stakeholders.

Human Resources

For many organizations, "human resource development" is just a renaming of old personnel functions, not a *development* of the human resources necessary for the long-term vitality of the organization.

Physical Facilities

This same lack of investment has typified far too many organizations when it comes to their physical facilities. Many businesses that are dependent on production or service facilities are much less competitive simply because they have not constantly reinvested in those facilities.

The Physical Facility

Technological Resources

The cost of staying technologically current is also significant. When organizations realize the water surrounding them is becoming hotter, they sometimes respond by limiting funds for necessary technological investments. A frequent result is that their competitors are more technologically advanced. This gap in technology makes successfully shaping the future even more problematic.

Competition

Another major barrier to shaping the future is the deepening competition in virtually every type of business. While the competition in heavy-manufacturing, consumer-electronics, and high-technology industries has increased dramatically over the past two decades, competition for dollars, clients, and personnel has also increased for those in other industries. Not-for-profit organizations are also facing the competitive stresses that are common among their counterparts in internationally competitive manufacturing operations. Available resources have declined, while needs have increased.

A further challenge confronting organization leaders is that competitors for the markets of the future are not standing still. It may be disheartening to identify current gaps between your organization and its competition. Nevertheless, it is even more anxiety provoking to realize that the competition is actively working to shape its future and, therefore, the gap between you and the competition will be wider tomorrow than it is today—unless you act quickly to shape your own future.

Inertia

One of the most significant barriers to successfully shaping the future of your organization is one that is almost invisible: *organizational inertia*. Borrowing from our friends in physics, we find that "a body in motion tends to stay in motion; a body at rest tends to stay at rest." In organizational life, one of the major barriers to successfully shaping the future of the organization is the tendency of an organization to continue to be as it has been. Without dramatic efforts, the best indicator of the next three years is likely the trends of the last three years. For organizations to succeed at shaping their own future, they must overcome the current patterns of behavior. This can take inordinate effort on the part of organizational leaders and others who would have the organization be different.

Overcoming Barriers

To successfully shape the future of your organization, you must overcome the many barriers that would inhibit this process. You must not approach the process of shaping the future as though it were a *sprint*. A sprint is a race to the finish, uninhibited by barriers. The emphasis is on a fast start and a burst of speed sustained until the goal of reaching the finish line is achieved. To win a sprint you condition yourself carefully before the race. During the race you go all out to reach the goal. The fastest, most effective runner wins this type of race.

The Creative Approach

Too many organizations approach shaping their future as though this process were a sprint. It clearly is not. Continuing this track-and-field analogy, we contend that the process of shaping your future is like a *hurdling* event. For the hurdles, athletes practice running toward the goal as fast as possible while leaping over predictable, fence-like hurdles. They know that these hurdles will be between them and the goal; therefore, they practice both jumping and running swiftly.

As you approach shaping your organization's future, plan on encountering hurdles before reaching your goal. This race is never a simple sprint. You must plan ahead to be able to leap over the hurdles or, if you are creative, go around them or under them. As you proceed with the process of shaping your future, you must be so committed to reaching your goal that you see the hurdles not as impenetrable barriers but as manageable challenges that you will meet. Then you must quickly continue in your race to achieve your organizational goals.

Finding Specific Solutions

As you examine the various barriers we have outlined, consider the specific things you might do to overcome some of these hurdles. For example, organizational inflexibility must be constantly questioned. You must become an advocate for reducing the rigidity of current structures and for developing flexible structures that will enable your organization to meet the constant challenges it will face.

Paradigms can be either significant barriers to your success or hurdles to leap over or circumvent. You must become a paradigm hunter. You must identify the paradigms in your industry, your organization, and the situation at hand. You must help members of the organization examine paradigms and determine which aspects of the paradigms are helpful and which are inhibiting your progress.

You must be comfortable with taking the risk of challenging assumptions deeply held by others. While it may make you both controversial and lonely, this behavior is one of the keys to breaking out of the limits of the past and enabling you and your organization to achieve its ideal future.

As we mentioned, the notion of "If it ain't broke, don't fix it" can be disastrous. Therefore, you must adopt the mentality captured in Robert Kriegel's book *If It Ain't Broke, Break It!* (1991). This book portrays the desirable spirit of the leaders who will successfully shape the future of their organizations. It presses the need to tackle important issues and opportunities early rather than waiting until later when the problems become much worse. It forces the organization to let go of that which seems comfortable and to seek to identify and achieve that which is most desirable for the future.

In many organizations, dealing with resource limits requires two important steps:

1. *Defining a future that has focus.* The era in which many new lines of business and many new markets could be pursued simultaneously is likely over. Your ideal future will need to involve fewer lines of business and fewer markets, thus allowing limited resources to be concentrated more carefully.

2. *Creatively leveraging the use of limited resources.* You may lease instead of purchase physical facilities. You may have to examine creative ways of financing the future of your organization. You may enter into alliances that help you overcome human resource limits—either in the development of criti-

cally important human resources or in the shared utilization of these key resources.

You may also have to be creative in achieving access to necessary technologies to enable you to achieve your ideal future. Creativity here may again take the form of strategic alliances, licensing arrangements, or an artful ability to swiftly and effectively imitate the technology leaders in your industry. In this era of limited resources, you will have to be deliberate as you seek effective solutions to the limits you will confront.

Fighting organizational inertia to get the organization to move in new directions requires hard work. You should plan for resistance to many of the changes proposed. Reviewing the section on resistance in Chapter 3 will help you prepare for resistance to even well-planned change, and you must do a great deal of work prior to launching any necessary change.

Another key factor in overcoming your organization's inertia is a whole-hearted commitment to successfully shaping the future. You cannot dabble at shaping the future. If you are tentative, organizational inertia will cancel out your efforts.

Understanding Change as an Ongoing, Holistic Process

Shaping the future of your organization is not an episodic event. It is not something you "do" and then are finished with. It is a constant, ongoing process, and you must approach it as such. An organization that is approaching change efforts is like a trapeze artist who must release one trapeze in order to successfully catch the next. The role of the leader/manager ("complete" leader) is to provide encouragement, timing, and a safety net for those who must let go of today's stability for tomorrow's opportunity.

The Complete Leader

This leader must also help people understand that grabbing the next trapeze is necessary but not sufficient for the long-term viability of the organization, because the change effort will be continual. There is no arrival point at which stability will be permanent. At best, you will find only a temporary stepping-off point for the next phase of this ongoing effort to create your successful future. This must be clear both to you and to those whom you would guide into the future.

Successfully shaping the future of an organization requires a holistic effort. Programs that seek to change just one or two aspects of an organization are doomed to failure — or, at best, mediocrity. When you change any given component of your organization, all other aspects of the organization will also change. One of the reasons that we have supplied you with a structure for this process—the

Applied Strategic Planning approach—is to give you a clear path to follow. It may also be helpful for you to use some model of organizational functioning to help you plan and track the impacts that a change in one area will have throughout the organization.

The Challenge Is Yours

We have identified the ten keys to success in shaping your organization's future, and we have endeavored to clearly define them and to recommend appropriate action. Applied Strategic Planning (Key 10) is an overarching tool to enable you to succeed in this process. We have identified, discussed, and provided solutions to the many barriers that you are likely to encounter in seeking to shape your organization's future.

As you have worked your way through these discussions, the issues you are facing should have become increasingly clear to you. You have also had an opportunity to examine some of the challenges confronting your organization. We hope that we have helped, but the challenge is yours. The question of whether you will commit to this effort can only be answered by you.

REFERENCES

Ackoff, R. *Creating the Corporate Future*. New York: John Wiley, 1981.

Barker, J. A. *Future Edge: Discovering the New Paradigms of Success*. New York: William Morrow, 1992.

Blanchard, K., and Johnson, S. *The One-Minute Manager*. New York: William Morrow, 1982.

Block, P. *The Empowered Manager: Positive Political Skills at Work*. San Francisco: Jossey-Bass, 1987.

Cetron, M. J., and Davies, O. *Crystal Globe: The Have and Have-Nots of the World Order*. New York: St. Martin's Press, 1991.

Drucker, P. F. *Managing for the Future: The 1990s and Beyond*. New York: Dutton, 1992.

Goodstein, L. D., and Burke, W. W. "Creating Successful Organizational Change," *Organizational Dynamics*, 1991, *19* (4), 5–17.

Goodstein, L. D., Nolan, T. M., and Pfeiffer, J. W. *Applied Strategic Planning: A Comprehensive Guide*. San Diego: Pfeiffer & Company, 1992.

Harrison, R., and Stokes, H. *Diagnosing Organizational Culture*. San Diego: Pfeiffer & Company, 1992.

Harvey, J. B. *The Abilene Paradox and Other Meditations on Management*. San Diego: Pfeiffer & Company, 1988.

Kouzes, J. M., and Posner, B. Z. *The Leadership Challenge: How to Get Extraordinary Things Done in Organizations*. San Francisco: Jossey-Bass, 1987.

Kriegel, R. *If It Ain't Broke, Break It!* New York: Warner Books, 1991.

Levitt, T. "Marketing Myopia," *Harvard Business Review*, July-August 1960, pp. 45–56. Reprinted in J. W. Pfeiffer (ed.), *Strategic Planning: Selected Readings*, rev. ed. San Diego: Pfeiffer & Company, 1991.

Lewin, K. *Field Theory in Social Science*. Westport, Conn.: Greenwood, 1975.

Linneman, R. E., and Stanton, J. L., Jr. *Making Niche Marketing Work*. New York: McGraw-Hill, 1991.

"Managers' Manager John Humphrey," *Inc.*, September 1987, pp. 49–58.

Naisbitt, J., and Aburdene, P. *Megatrends 2000: Ten New Directions for the 1990s.* New York: William Morrow, 1990.

Schein, E. *Organizational Culture and Leadership.* San Francisco: Jossey-Bass, 1985.

Sculley, J., and Byrne, J. A. *Odyssey: Pepsi to Apple.* New York: Harper & Row.

Senge, P. M. *The Fifth Discipline: The Art and Practice of the Learning Organization.* New York: Doubleday, 1990.

Viscott, D. *Risking.* New York: Simon & Schuster, 1977.

ADDITIONAL READING

Badarasco, J. L., Jr. *The Knowledge Link*. Boston: Harvard Business School Press, 1991.

Davis, S., and Davidson, B. *2020 Vision*. New York: Simon & Schuster, 1991.

Kouzes, J. M., and Posner, B. Z. *The Leadership Challenge: How to Get Extraordinary Things Done in Organizations*. San Francisco: Jossey-Bass, 1987.

INDEX

173

Editors:
Mary Kitzmiller
JoAnn Padgett

Editorial Assistants:
Katharine A. Munson
Steffany N. Perry

Cover:
John Odam Design Associates

Page Composition:
Paul Bond

Illustrator:
David Hills, Ph.D.